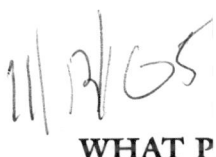

WHAT P

"New Decision Therapy is an extraordinary approach to healing! Kandis Blakely has written a very valuable book filled with life-changing information! I have witnessed her program having a profound healing effect on people—physically, mentally and spiritually."
—Pamala Oslie, *Your Life Colors*, Santa Barbara, CA

"This little book takes you by surprise. It triggers unconscious memories. It is a Wake-Up Call. Perhaps if each of us read and used the tools offered in this neatly packaged technique, we would not need to suffer heart attacks and other dramas to remind us of the highest and purest teachings ever brought forth: Forgiveness, Compassion, Acceptance, and Love."
—Dana Conant, Mt. Shasta, CA

"This book directly addresses the emotional component of disease. A precise method of intervention. It is a very helpful book."
—Max Steiner, MD

"I've been using NDT with a small group of clients and having profound results. One of them said what we have all felt, 'It feels honest; not a trick'."
—Melanie Clark, MFCC, San Francisco, CA

"Kandis' work frees people from the tyranny of their thoughts."
—Alexander James, LSW, Missoula, MT

"Kandis' work is a powerful way for people to heal past hurts. By quickly pinpointing a belief that is no longer serving them and by a loving process of release, individuals are lead to made a 'new decision,' which changes their perception of the past, and provides a springboard from which a person can live a happier life."
—Rev. Sally Rutis, *Living Enrichment Center*, Oregon

"It (NDT) is quick, permanent psychological surgery. It changed my life. I am no longer controlled by my past!"
—Nancy Harkness, CEO, Houston, TX

"Kandis is the most revolutionary of all teachers. Others are merely scratching the surface, rearranging unimportant externals. She goes to the root of things and removes that."
—Carolyn Theill, MS, Kona, HI

"Since learning this technique, I have been amazed at watching 'old programs' go by without my having to participate in them anymore."
—Timothy Schulz, MA, Yakima, WA

"I am a teacher and a therapist who had tried everything—and still felt my life force draining away. At some point I made a decision to die. NDT located that point in time and cleared it from my Being. THIS IS IT!"
—Alicia Woods, Santa Fe, NM

"A woman came to see me feeling depressed and suicidal. Over the past year she had broken her hip, survived skin cancer and her partner died in a plane crash. After a *single NDT session*, her resolve to live was so strong that she started a new business and reconnected with her family, saying 'I want to live!'"
—Zae Zatoon, PhD, Kona, HI

"As a practicing physician in Family Practice, I can highly recommend New Decision Therapy. It is something worth trying before considering any surgery. You may be surprised at how much good it does for you!"
—Kinnie McCabe, MD, Seattle, WA

"NDT is providing me and my clients a new framework for addressing therapeutic issues and—even more valuable—a new language that resonates with body wisdom."
—Barbara Douglas, WA

"One of the best successes was a lady on morphine for cancer pain. She had a tumor around her kidney. The cancer was the kind that spreads fast when exposed to air and was therefore inoperable. Two weeks after her NDT work, she was declared 'cancer free.'"
—Sally Brunell, MS, Salem, OR

"A fantastically real, truthful, shorthand form of therapy that gets to the deepest issues without trauma."
—Capt. Merlyn Erickson, CRNA, Anchorage, AK

"Kandis uses her heart, mind and all of her senses to identify and release core emotional issues that burden everyone's system. I have used NDT since the workshop with deep and lasting results. I was surprised to uncover and delighted to release core issues in myself despite hundreds of hours of other therapies and workshops."
—Dr. Linda Fickes, DC, Oahu, HI

Say you are watching a video and get to a part where you are so involved you even stop blinking. Then the doorbell rings. You put the movie on pause. Then the telephone rings. The children come home, etc. *The video is still on pause until you release it.*

The same kind of experience happens in our emotional life. Traumatic events occur. If the experience is not released, the disturbing energy is held within our body, arresting life force energy, wellness and joy. A reminder from one of our senses triggers unconscious memory and the trauma is re-experienced in some form.

Through the use of the New Decision Therapy™ process, we can go back to the time when we put that part of our movie on pause.

We can free ourselves and others from the tyranny of this hold...

New Decision Therapy™ can be used as a valuable self-help technique. Initially, however, it is essential to work with a certified NDT™ practitioner to thoroughly clear core emotional issues.

For information on certified practitioners, see Appendix F.

YOUR BODY REMEMBERS

A Conscious Choice to Live

Kandis Blakely, MFCC

Cover and page design by Quicksilver Productions, Mt. Shasta, CA.

Cover photograph by Jaya, Inner Light Photography, Big Sur, CA.

ATHERIKA PRODUCTIONS
P. O. Box 1091
Mt. Shasta, CA 96067
U.S.A.

Security is mostly a superstition.
It does not exist in nature,
nor do the children of men as a whole
experience it.
Avoiding danger is no safer in the long run
than outright exposure.
Life is either a daring adventure, or nothing.
To keep our faces toward change and
behave like free spirits in the presence of fate
is strength undefeatable.

—Helen Keller, *Let Us Have Faith* (1940)

ACKNOWLEDGEMENTS

I wish to thank God, my mother and father, my children, and all the people who have trusted me and were willing to do New Decision Therapy and follow their true paths.

YOUR BODY REMEMBERS

CONTENTS

NDT: A Contribution to Medicine
We can only heal that to which we have become conscious. There is a tragic flaw—you cannot avoid it. You must live its lesson consciously.

Letting Go and Going On
You do not outgrow a life-negating decision. You must make an archaeological dig and find decisive moments in your life. New Decision Therapy enters into your system and breaks the cycle.

12 Steps to Making a Conscious Choice To Live
Stay conscious in the present moment. You are making Life Decisions all the time. This is not a dress rehearsal. This is your life.

Manifesting Your Desires
What feeds you? What depletes you? Thoughts have energy. Your body listens to your mind. Your body registers your emotions.

PREFACE TO 2ND EDITION

D id you know that your body is surrounded by an electromagnetic energy field? Thoughts travel into this energy field, attracting a state of health created by your beliefs. A predisposition to health comes from harmonious adaptation from birth throughout childhood and into adulthood. Your core beliefs directly affect your immune system.

The information in this book is based on the belief that your body tells the truth. Your physical body registers every thought, feeling and experience. You can learn to decode valuable information from your body.

The fundamental dilemma today is psychological amnesia. You forget events and feelings and experiences. This forgetting stands between you and your birthright of health and well-being. You need only remember.

A human being repeats until he remembers all of himself. If you want to know your past, look at yourself today. If you want to know your future, look at yourself today. Your past comes into your present to remind you of your future. This is the ultimate mind-body connection.

This book tells you how to clear past traumas and create an impeccable relationship with yourself. You can clear out the hurts of the past and bring your complete self into focus. Once this primary relationship with self is launched, relationships with others take on new meaning. Rather than filling in the blanks to complete yourself, you are ready to meet with other whole individuals.

New Decision Therapy™ is a *Conscious Choice to Live.* NDT™ asks your body to remember and release past traumas and the people associated with the pain. NDT uses contemporary psychology and applied kinesiology. The body is asked when it got stuck. The trauma is looked at and unlocked.

New Decision Therapy asks: What does your soul want in order to heal? Memories create your physical body. Cellular memory holds pattern for disease and wellness. In order for you to set up a new vibrational fluctuation in the cells of your body, you have to consciously communicate with material that has been in your unconscious mind. Each memory is created and maintained by your emotions and each emotion has two components: 1) a thought; and 2) a physical sensation.

The effectiveness of NDT is due to its ability to bring your thoughts from a hidden memory into consciousness. True healing gets rid of the memory of an illness on a cellular level. In this way, the memory ceases to recreate itself.

The intent of this book is to transport you *consciously* from an environment of fear to a place of faith. Fear masquerades as anger and guilt. After thorough emotional clearing, a plethora of toxic anger and guilt is effectively released. This leaves space for the nurturing of faith.

As we near the end of the twentieth century, we humans are quite sophisticated examples of mental technology and physical refinement. While our minds and bodies are models of highly developed resources, our emotions are often stunted. They are frequently developmentally arrested at a chronological age far younger than our biological age. This point of emotional arrested development is in a specific moment in time.

The technique used in New Decision Therapy facilitates the release of previously unexpressed emotions that are tied to significant events in the past. Perhaps the loss of a loved one, the loss of a cherished phase of your life, or the loss of a personal hope or dream.

This exquisite therapy then goes one step further. It helps you to reconstruct your life based on a happy and healthy choice to be Fully Alive. NDT suggests that health is a state of mental, emotional and physical harmony. New Decision Therapy takes you to this harmonic.

The time is Now. You must let go of past atrocities in order to Live Freely. Letting go of past horrors requires consciousness. Recall. Remembering is the first step. Forgiveness is learning to walk.

Forgiveness must be genuine. It must be authentic. It cannot be real until you embrace specific traumas with conscious understanding.

I became disheartened by traditional psychotherapy with its focus on analysis. Many people would spend years getting in touch with and spewing their anger but never truly clearing it. They were leaving their therapists' office pounding out their anger and taking other people hostage while they were going through their "process." Some fortunate ones would eventually come to a point of forgiveness and acceptance. The journey was long and tedious. Few had sufficient discipline and dedication to get to the other side of their pain.

New Decision Therapy is *fast*. It identifies specific traumas and uproots them quickly. It is psychosurgery.

This book must be read by everybody who enters the human race. Nobody is impervious to its message.

New Decision Therapy is not another Quick Fix in an age of instant everything, from breakfast to divorce. It is not another unconscious distraction desiring immediate gratification. This is Quantum Healing. The alchemy happens in the moment of conscious remembering.

This book offers an explanation of a profound psychological surgery. Everyone can benefit from it. The results catapult you into a new level of growth and acceptance.

INTRODUCTION

Who am I?

First and foremost, I am a human being. I am a part of All that has ever been and ever will be. I am just like you. And, like you, I am Unique.

Secondly, I am a woman, a girl, a child, someone's daughter, a mother, and a grandmother. I am a partner to a wonderful man. I am a friend. I am a co-worker to therapists, doctors, caregivers, publishers, and a whole world of marketing engineers.

I am also a teacher. I teach what I know. And, I teach what I need to know. I teach what I have learned. And, I teach what I need to learn.

I am an author. And so I bring you this book.

I was born in Brooklyn, New York. I lived there with my immediate and somewhat celebrated extended family. At age three I was transplanted to the suburbs of New Jersey, the "Garden State" of the east coast.

I was a tomboy. That was the closest I could replicate to being a real boy. So it had to do. Athletic activities brought me closer to Dad, and though I was an organized housekeeper, I only came to Mom's rescue when one or both of us were desperate for a connection. The bond was weak. Neither of us had the resources to be emotionally available.

As I entered puberty, I made my first conscious decision about being female. It went something like this: "Boys have more freedom and therefore more fun... girls are weak and live with the threat of lurking danger." I then forgot about this decision.

The activation of this early decision manifested for me about ten years later. I had spent a decade enjoying the liberties of being a single, college-educated young lady with a self-designed lifestyle in Greenwich Village, New York. I was on scholarship to a dance theater performing arts company. I walked where and when I wanted. I was light and filled with hope about my future. I was happy and cheerful, believing that my life was laced with good fortune.

At age 24 I gave birth to my first daughter. Healthy and enthusiastic, I quickly returned to my home in Philadelphia to enjoy a walk in the early fall weather. As I proudly (and carefully) held my little girl to my breast, a young neighborhood boy snatched my purse. It contained all my medical and financial assets. I was devastated.

I panicked because I felt helpless. I was a female. I had a baby in my arms. I could not grab my purse from the boy and I couldn't chase after him. I was self-pronounced "vulnerable in the first degree." I instantly became that 14-year-old girl who bought the lie that she was helpless in a male dominated world. They (the boys) were stronger and faster. *I was not enough.*

It took a traumatic event to ignite an old decision born of a lie. I did not have the tools to recognize or clear that trauma. It became part of my outlook on life. Fear took over. I lived in fear at times when I needed to live in love.

So I compensated. I developed many skills (and defenses) under the heading of "independence." I trusted less; I separated more. The worst part was I didn't have a clue as to my motivation. I was operating out of unconscious drives, out of darkness. I did not even know the lights were out.

By age 29, I had a master's degree in dance and was a college instructor. At 31, I gave birth to my second daughter. Physical weaknesses led me to seek medical assistance. Perhaps this was the most traumatic experience of all. Traditional medicine is sorely lacking in inspiration. It's as if the professionals are reluctant to offer hope, afraid the medicine won't deliver. Faith, Trust and Courage have somehow been lost. Ironically, these are the ingredients that activate our will to live, therefore strengthening our immune system.

Alternative medical modalities realize the incompleteness of modern medicine. In attempting to get results, they have tried to force feed spirituality. The problem is many practitioners brought their own perceived separation from God into their practice. Until we heal our emotional wounds from the past and reconnect consciously to the Source, we can only pass on partial truths and our own doubts.

In search of my own physical wellness, I visited massage therapists, acupuncturists, chiropractors and nutritionists. I read a lot of books on food imbalances. I identified with everything. As I received help from a particular treatment, I was so grateful that I wanted to share my new knowledge with everyone who was suffering. I went to school. I took exams. I secured degrees and accumulated licenses. And, I still didn't know why people weren't truly and deeply changing for the better.

Today, I can say, "I've been there, done that, got the degree and the license."

I used to wonder...

...**as a Massage Therapist**, why can't my clients "let go" (of their past hurts)?

...**in Chiropractic School,** why don't adjustments hold?

...**doing Nutritional Programs,** why do people stop taking their supplements? Why do they continue eating refined sugar?

...**as a Psychotherapist,** why don't my clients "go on" with their lives?

...**as a Conscious Person,** why can't everyone "be present"?

There was really only one response:
BECAUSE THEY CAN'T!

They would if they could.

1. They are stuck.
2. They have forgotten the moment in time when "their lights went out."
3. They can't find the light switch.
4. In an attempt to remember, they repeat similar insults.
5. They believe "nothing changes."

I dedicated myself to discovering "why" and developing a "how to" program. It required a fundamental change in consciousness. This little book offers you the result of that quest.

Kandis Blakely, MFCC

Your thoughts are

the basic

building blocks

of your

Physical Reality.

CHAPTER ONE

YOU ARE WHAT YOU THINK

Thoughts Have Great Power

Your thoughts and beliefs affect every aspect of your life and every cell in your body. What you consciously and unconsciously think and believe has such a profound effect on you that it can weaken or strengthen your body's immune system.

The essence of your being is a field of awareness that interacts with itself and becomes both mind and body. You are a consciousness which conceives, governs, constructs and actually becomes the mind and the body. This faculty of inner awareness, when cultivated, causes the dramatic change from chaos to calm, from illness to health.

99.9% of Our Body is Empty Space

According to physicists, the empty space of our bodies is composed of non-material fluctuations of energy and information. Just as a quantum unit of light is a photon, the quantum unit of the mind-body interaction is a thought. This thought can be a feeling, desire, instinct or concept. This non-verbal impulse of information comes from our consciousness.

Neuropeptides are chemical substances that are made and released by brain cells. They are actually molecules that send messages all over the body. They float through the body fluids and are attracted to specific receptors in the body. Neuropeptides and their receptors grow directly off of the cell structure (DNA). They create an information network, a communication system. When the receptor sites receive the neuropeptides, a change occurs in the DNA, the physical cellular structure.

> As we think, we are making molecules, and these molecules are being generated not only in our mind or in our brain cells, they are being generated in our whole body. To think is to practice brain chemistry... When we have a thought or a feeling or an emotion, then in our brains we make a set of chemicals known as neuropeptides (*neuro*, because they are found in the brain; *peptides* because they are protein-like molecules)... A brain cell, when it wants to talk to another brain cell, manufactures these neuropeptides that then go and latch onto the receptor sites of the other brain cells.[1]

Most neuropeptides alter behavior and mood states. Receptors to these neuropeptides are also found on monocytes, T-cells and B-cells, which are mobile cells

[1] Chopra, Deepak, Dr., *Magical Mind Magical Body*, Nightingale Conant audio series

of the immune system. The thymus produces "T" cells, or thymus derived cells, which are part of the army of white blood cells that protect the system from foreign invasion. They recognize and attack foreign materials that are life threatening and protect the genetic identity of the body. "Neuropeptides and their receptors thus join the brain, glands and immune system in a network of communication between brain and body, probably representing the biochemical substrata of emotion."[2] The thymus gland monitors thought. Consequently, *your thymus is monitoring every conscious or unconscious thought you have.* If there is a life-negating thought, that thought suppresses the thymus and the immune system will not function properly.

Illness Can Be Physical, Mental Or Emotional

According to former NASA scientist, Barbara Brennan,

> Illness can be seen as simply a message from your body to you that says, *Wait a minute; something is wrong. You are not listening to your whole self; you are ignoring something very important to you. What is it?* The source of the illness needs to be searched for in this way, either on the psychological or feeling level, on the level of understanding or simply by a change in one's state of being, which may not be conscious. A return to health requires much more personal work and change than simply taking pills prescribed by a doctor. Without personal change you will eventually create another problem to lead you back to the source that

---

[2] Pert, Candace, Dr. (of National Institute of Mental Health), Journal of Immunology, 1985

caused the disease in the first place. I have found that the source is the key. To deal with the source usually requires a life change that ultimately leads to a personal life more connected to the core of one's being.[3]

Illness begins with a thought. The more serious the illness, the more deeply it is connected to the mental process. A person with a life-threatening illness may be fulfilling an unconscious decision to die. By using the tools of Applied Kinesiology (AK) and Behavioral Kinesiology (BK) we are now able to determine that such a decision has been made, and pinpoint the exact time and incident that precipitated the decision.

Your Body Remembers

Using Applied and Behavioral Kinesiology, your body will provide accurate yes or no responses to specific questions. Consequently, you can ask the body, *What does this illness mean to you? When did this illness take over? What was the thought that preceded the diagnosis?* The body provides details as if it were a personal diary in which the most intimate, minute data of your life are stored. Through the use of Applied and Behavioral Kinesiology, your body accesses every memory and thought form you have ever had. With the use of BK we can determine that an illness may be fulfilling a thought, *If this is what life is about, I don't want to live.*

A decision of this complexity is usually operating on an unconscious level. Consciously, a person may be

---

[3] Brennan, Barbara, *Hands of Light, A Guide to Healing Through the Human Energy Field*, Pleiades Books, New York, 1987

unaware of their choice to die. They may even be making concerted efforts toward their healing. The sad fact, however, is that a person with a death wish will inadvertently choose ineffective methods of self-repair. They may sabotage their attempts to be healthy. For example, Willard, an accountant with a law firm, was suffering from a general malaise that left him exhausted much of the time. His first medical diagnosis was Epstein-Barr Virus. Upon seeking a second opinion, he was told that he had a vitamin deficiency. A third physician found no symptoms and suggested that it was all in Willard's head. Although the second physician's diagnosis was correct, Willard did not follow his advice and chose to accept the diagnosis of the first doctor. The first doctor suggested that he sleep more and drink at least eight glasses of water a day, neither of which Willard did. He was also given pills to alleviate his symptoms, which he repeatedly forgot to take. Until Willard was able to release his unconscious decision to die several months later, he continued his path of self-sabotage.

Past Decisions Determine Present Actions

Past decisions are continuously being acted out in the present moment. If one of these life decisions is an unconscious death wish, it too is currently being activated. It is frightening to think that an unconscious death wish may be in charge of your life. In order to stop this momentum, a New Decision must be made. A conscious choice to live, of equal intensity, must be made to meet and clear the charge of a life-negating decision.

The Repetition Compulsion

We are constantly making choices. However, we are not always aware of the deep inner feelings that dictate or influence our behavioral choices. If we unconsciously harbor negative feelings such as fear, despair and resentment, we tend to inadvertently manifest similar experiences that cause us to re-experience these deep inner feelings. Dr. Sigmund Freud, considered to be the father of psychoanalysis, spoke of this as the repetition compulsion. He suggested that we repeat until we remember. This repetition proceeds in a vicious cycle. The only way to break the cycle is to bring our unconscious intentions into conscious awareness.

From many years of clinical experience I found that we repeat self-negating patterns in a desperate attempt to reclaim a piece of ourselves that is buried in our unconscious mind. Our repetition is really an effort to have that buried piece surface and be recognized. We repeat a particular scenario until we have excruciating clarity in the depths of our lives. In an effort to remember we find ourselves setting up similar circumstances so that we can re-experience the buried feelings from our past. When we have stirred up the old feelings, the conscious mind begins to recognize emotional patterns.

Denial And Psychological Amnesia

We often forget past decisions. Denial simply means that the conscious mind cannot access the unconscious experience. Sometimes we forget our decisions because the circumstances surrounding a particular event are too painful to recall. In this instance, the mind suppresses the information, removing the feelings of hurt from the forefront of our lives or conscious awareness. The body, however, remembers. As an example, Emma's husband, Edward, died quite suddenly. He had suffered a heart attack in the physician's office while having a checkup and died in the hospital five days later. Emma had been able to cope with Edward's heart attack and virtually lived at the hospital for the next four days. She finally went home, at Edward's insistence, to take some time out. That night Edward passed on. It wasn't until eight years later that Emma accessed the decision she had made when she received the phone call informing her of Edward's death, which was, *I don't want to live without you. I want to go, too.*

Another reason we are not in conscious contact with some decisions is due to "input overload." This is when there are too many message units for the brain to process. And although we may try to put them out of our conscious minds, we are often still attached to the energy in these thoughts. Randy, a full time massage therapist, was taking courses towards a master's degree at a local university. His son Derrick, who was too young for a drivers license, wrecked their only car on the same day as Randy's final exam. Earlier that same day his wife, Susan, informed him she was pregnant with their third child. Randy had just left his last client and was on the way to take his exam when he fell off his bicycle and broke his foot, thereby missing his exam. Five years later his foot had still not healed properly. It was while undergoing foot surgery that Randy remembered his decision. Five years before, he had thought, *I don't want to take another step, I can't go on. This is too much for me.*

Decisions Can Be Preverbal

A third reason we forget our decisions is because they occurred at a preverbal stage of our lives. Since we don't have the skills to speak our mind as infants, we put our thoughts on hold until we have the words to talk about them. A dancer named Wendy had been premature at birth. She had to be taken from her mother and placed in a special "preemie" tank where she was left alone for much of the following eight weeks. She experienced devastating feelings of abandonment. Wendy did not possess the verbal skills to express her distress. As an adult, she attracted relationships that left her abandoned. Her unconscious mind encouraged her to repeat emotional scenarios in hopes of awakening her conscious mind. Once she consciously remembered the initial pain and accompanying fear, she began to heal the old wound.

Every Memory Is Held In Your Body

Everything you have ever seen or learned has a cellular imprint. Old hurts, both physical and emotional, are stored in your cells. Past memories can be activated in the present by circumstances, sounds, smells, etc. One advertising agency had planned an office fire drill and the alarm went off at the appointed time. Kelly, a young executive of the firm, suddenly and inexplicably became panic stricken. She later had the memory of when she was in the sixth grade and broke the little glass arm off the fire alarm activator which set off the alarm. Because of this incident she was sent to the principal's office. She remembered how ashamed she felt for causing havoc and getting in trouble, which triggered a sense of panic. Her inappropriate reaction to the office fire alarm was that of a frightened, panic-stricken child, even though she hadn't done anything wrong.

We must become conscious. As we clear past hurts, fears, shame, and anger, we can begin to live now. The only thing we can do about the past is clean it up. Our aliveness is in this moment. As we clear up our history, we begin to live fully in the present.

Conscious Choices

When we step out of denial, we begin to make conscious choices. We begin to hear ourselves and open our heart space. We begin to act with clear, focused and creative intent. In the present, we have the opportunity to be whole. We can have meaningful experiences and special human encounters each moment. It is refreshing and revitalizing. Change is constantly taking place within us.

With compassionate understanding and forgiveness of past circumstances, we begin to clear and heal emotionally. Since the past has been honored and put to rest, the old associations are complete. This emotional cleansing allows us to live with joy and lightheartedness.

Emotional Homework

Many people are developing their minds without doing any emotional clearing. This keeps communication between our conscious intentions and their unconscious drives blocked. People have forgotten what it is to be human. We act like programmed machines using various coping skills and addictions to maintain a lifestyle. Most addictions are born of fear and superstition. These fear-based addictions inhibit our full creative self expression. While they serve us as survival tools, they do not leave room for new creative experiences. An addiction can cause a person to go out of balance. If a person is so addicted to their routine, they may become irritable or frightened if their usual routine is interrupted. A person needs to be free of fearful dogma in order to allow space for adventure and miracles.

You are in Fear or You are in Love

Addictive attachments are born of fear. Fear is very limiting. Love, on the other hand, is an expanded state. When you are in love, your creativity flows. It is your natural condition. You simply let go of your addictions because they no longer serve you. You begin to choose freely. Your actions now come from your true self. This is the Self which was lost during times of betrayal, humiliation, abandonment and rejection.

Doubt and Worry

Doubt depresses your Life Energy. It feeds on the lie of separation. Your doubt blocks the doorway of conscious connection with all of humanity. Moreover, the action of worry in your mind transfers into a heaviness in your body. Negative emotions block the flow of physical energy.

The Wake-Up Call

We must remember. A truly effective therapeutic intervention puts consciousness back in the cells so that we can begin to remember. By bringing our intentions into consciousness, we begin to open up our memory bank and break the cycle. Decisions made in the past become conscious. When our choices are based on love in the present, rather than past fear, we are operating from truth. The process of becoming authentic begins with the opening and clearing of the emotional body. It is time to take responsibility for our intentions. It is time to be conscious of what we are feeling and the actions we are taking.

Life Force

maintains the

positive and negative

Balance

of the Universe

in a powerful

and harmonious

Rhythm.

CHAPTER TWO

THE *LIFE FORCE*

There is an electromagnetic energy field that radiates out from the human body. Everything you think, feel and do reflects in this field. "Each of us generates a self surrounding, ultra high frequency, electromagnetic field, exquisitely ephemeral but exquisitely real."[1] This field is sustained by our *Life Force*. It keeps our hearts beating. It is the energy, ch'i or prana that maintains every living organism.

The Human Aura

Dr. Valerie Hunt, a neurophysiologist formerly at U.C.L.A., has documented that there is a field of energy which extends several feet out from the body and vibrates at 200,000 Hz (cycles per second). This is also known as the human aura. Because this field extends outside the body, it picks up information faster than the brain does. If somebody walked into the room, your field would pick up their presence more quickly than your brain would.[2]

------

[1] Fuller, Buckminster, Critical Path, 1981

[2] Kenyon, T., Acoustical Brain Research

Life Force is a vital energy that reveals itself in the material world as the laws of physics. It combines and coordinates matter in a rhythm with the Universe. When this energy enters the spiritual sphere, it is seen as reason, conscience and impulses. It is the basis of the psychic phenomena known as man.

Ch'i

In ancient Greece, philosophers referred to a force known as *pneuma*. Pneuma is presumed to manifest attributes of a god who transcends both matter and space. The ancient Greeks believed that, when pneuma was present in a body, that body was alive, and when pneuma was absent, that body was dead.

According to Chinese theory, the acupuncture points on the human body are points along an unseen meridian and vessel system (channels) that run deeply throughout the tissues of the body. These channels carry an invisible nutritive energy known to the Chinese as "ch'i" *(Life Force)*. This *Life Force* energy enters the body through the acupuncture points and flows to deeper organ structures, bringing life-giving nourishment of a subtle energetic nature. The Chinese have determined that there are six pairs of meridians and two vessels, known collectively as channels, that are connected to specific organ systems deep within the human structure. They have also found that when the flow of energy to the organs becomes blocked or imbalanced, dysfunction of the organ system will occur.

The meridian system forms a *physical-etheric* interface. One frequency band or octave in the aura that is just beyond the physical body is the etheric energy (or body).

It vibrates at speeds beyond light velocity and is magnetic in character. Bioenergetic information and vital energy move from the etheric body to the cellular level of the physical body via this meridian system.

The Astral Body

A second frequency band in the aura that vibrates at a different frequency than the etheric is the astral. The astral body is the individual field or vehicle of *feeling*, and as such it acts as a bridge between the mind and the physical body.

> The astral domain has certain unique properties, one of which is the principle that astrally or emotionally charged thoughts have a life of their own. At the astral energetic level, certain thoughts, either conscious or unconscious, may exist as distinct energy fields or thoughtforms with unique shapes, colors, and characteristics. Some thoughts, especially those that are charged with *emotional intensity*, can have a separate identity apart from their creator. Certain thoughts may actually be charged with subtle energetic substance and exist (unconsciously) as thoughtforms in the energetic fields of their creators. These thoughtforms can frequently be seen by clairvoyant individuals who are very sensitive to higher energetic phenomena. The fact that our consciousness can influence the energy fields of our subtle energetic anatomy has important implications for both medicine and psychology.

Subtle matter, especially astral matter, is very magnetic... One of the discoveries that researchers in psychology and medicine will eventually make some day is that *nonferrous matter also has the magnetic properties as ferrous matter. This includes the matter which goes into the substance of human thought and feeling.* It is not the type of magnetism which attracts iron filings. It does, however, react to electromagnetic fields. It attracts other substances in harmony with it, as well as repelling matter which is not in harmony with it. Experiments will eventually find that emotions must be dealt with both as highly magnetic nonphysical matter and as an aspect of consciousness. *The difficulty in treating many emotional illnesses stems, in part, from the fact that the emotions which cause these problems tend to be magnetically responsive to a kind of astral matter which easily "glues" itself both to our own feelings and to more of its own kind. The magnetic action makes it very difficult to get rid of the "bad" astral matter—and the emotional problem.* (emphasis added)[3]

The Will to Live

When a person makes a life-negating decision, this decision is immediately accompanied by a devastating loss of *Life Force*. Thoughts travel into our energy fields (astral body), and attract a particular state of health. A

---

[3] Leichtmen, R., *Einstein Returns* (Columbus, OH: Ariel Press, 1982), pp. 48-49

predisposition toward health comes from harmonious adaptation to particular circumstances from birth, through childhood and into adulthood.

Contrary to this adaptation principle is the popular theory that we harbor a death wish. It postulates that we have a "psychotic bit" or saboteur that wants to get rid of us. It may not be all of us but it is a piece of us that is in a self-destruct mode. It is the part of us that wants to die more than we want to live.

Life Force can be diminished, even depleted, by our reactions to significant events in our lives. Most of the time we are able to cope with these events or situations which may even have been dreadful enough to take us mentally or emotionally over the edge. We repair those gray areas, either because something good happens or we have an epiphany. We have our moment with God. We have a feeling of gratitude. Faith overcomes fear. Gratitude and courage overcome the insecurities, and we keep on going. We pick ourselves up, dust ourselves off and proceed with the next chapter of our lives.

The Last Straw

Sometimes, however, there is an event, situation or moment from which we don't recover. That event can weaken our *Life Force* enough to disturb the immune system. No matter what happened up to that particular moment in time, we still chose health and aliveness. From that moment on, no matter what happened, we followed the saboteur inside of us. This unconscious saboteur helped us find the wrong husband, the wrong physician, the wrong direction for our well-being. This moment of self defeat is triggered by an incident referred to as the *last straw*. It might not be the worst moment but it is the one when a person says, "I've had enough." The situation triggered a feeling of humiliation or shame or anger or betrayal or loss. In this instance a person may make a decision to give up on their life. Consciously or unconsciously they decide, *If this is what my life is about, I'd rather be dead*. The individual is then operating from a life-negating decision. In this case they are (unconsciously at least) sabotaging their health and happiness. They are making daily choices based on a core belief that their life is not worth living.

We live in shades of enthusiasm, but it is the black holes, the denials, that require conscious identification and release. Emotions that we are already identifying, acknowledging and releasing are part of our human experience. The emotions that we deny, store and become unconscious of are the ones that will control us. These thoughts will ultimately manifest as emotional attitudes and physical disease. If we don't bring these emotions into consciousness, they will get our attention some other way. If we fail to hear the whisper of that part of ourselves that is in pain, then perhaps the harsh reality of a failed gall bladder will do it. Will a person need a surgical bypass to open up their heart? They can let go of anger and choose forgiveness or suffer the possibility of a heart attack.

Unconscious Decisions

Therapeutic interventions can raise the consciousness of the individual who is suffering in order to enlighten them about their choices and decisions. Only after carefully exposing their unconscious motives can a person begin to explore the circumstances that precipitated their decisions. With fresh awareness of how and why their decisions were made, they have the opportunity to make a new, life-enhancing choice.

Many unconscious decisions that are running our lives were made when we were uninformed and unempowered. An early adaptive decision is frequently made with considerable anxiety, anger and resentment. It is also made without understanding or complete information. When we were young and we had a mommy, daddy or caretaker, we really needed them. We couldn't live without them. We would have remained cold, wet and hungry without them. We were so happy to have them that we took whatever they gave us. These guardians were coming from their dysfunctions and giving us what they had, as limited as that may have been. Our greatest need was to have an authentic, responsible, clear mirror in our first 18 months. This clean foundation would have then allowed us to accept ourselves totally, regardless of the bumps we received from society. Instead, our early caretakers often passed on their unedited emotional dispositions. Often, these attitudes were tainted.

We took the love from our parents but this came with all of their hang-ups and all of their incomplete "stuff." As a consequence, if they felt bad about themselves, we took on that poor self image. If they felt that they weren't good enough or that they were ugly or they were stupid, they imprinted that on us, too. We did not have the discernment as infants or toddlers to know that it was theirs, not ours.

We worked hard to be what we thought other people wanted us to be. We were unable to see ourselves. In a desperate attempt to ease our feelings of isolation, we looked to everybody else to see who we were. Our lives became a constant struggle to find ourselves.

In the past we made compromising decisions in order to make our lives easier. The long term effects of these decisions are usually just the opposite. By not being true to our authentic selves, we distort our bodies and create physiological disharmony. It is these chronic distortions that can cause tissue deterioration, heart disease, ulcers, arthritis and atrophied muscles, as well as shorten our natural life span. Distortions in mental attitudes weaken *Life Force*. Initially, the mind has a thought, the thymus hears the thought and sends energy to the physical body. When the thought is, *My life doesn't work and I don't want to live*, energy blocks begin to occur. The negative life decision becomes apparent when a person continues to be weakened by a chronic disease. A person's attitude is the largest contributing factor to their personal health. Our thoughts and predispositions determine our response to the transient, unpredictable phenomena we call our lives.

We are experts at feeling not okay. Feeling not okay comes from acting in thoughtless duplication of others, borrowing their attitudes about things, people and life. When a person feels okay, they do not feel compelled to produce adaptive behavior in order to maintain the status quo. They do not need to placate for fear of being rejected. What is left is spontaneous, congruent interactions with one's internal and external environment.

The First Step

is to become conscious

of your

thoughts and decisions.

Then,

Know the difference

between transient beliefs

and Fundamental

Core Decisions.

CHAPTER THREE

HEALTH BEGINS WITH AN ATTITUDE

Disease Can Be Reversed

In order to be truly healthy we must first recognize our negative mental attitudes and then transform them. A negative mental attitude is the first step in a downward spiral of a debilitating illness. The disease process can be reversed by altering the attitude or predisposing mental patterns. In cases of recurring illness it appears the patient has not made the underlying mental change necessary to strengthen the vulnerable area of their body. The word "incurable" simply means that the particular condition cannot be altered by using conventional medicine. In order to create health, we must go within to understand the emotional basis of our illness. The immune system can be strengthened by making a conscious choice to live.

Our Beliefs Create Our Attitudes

Our beliefs about health affect our immune system. Three major beliefs underly every life-negating attitude.

Figure 1

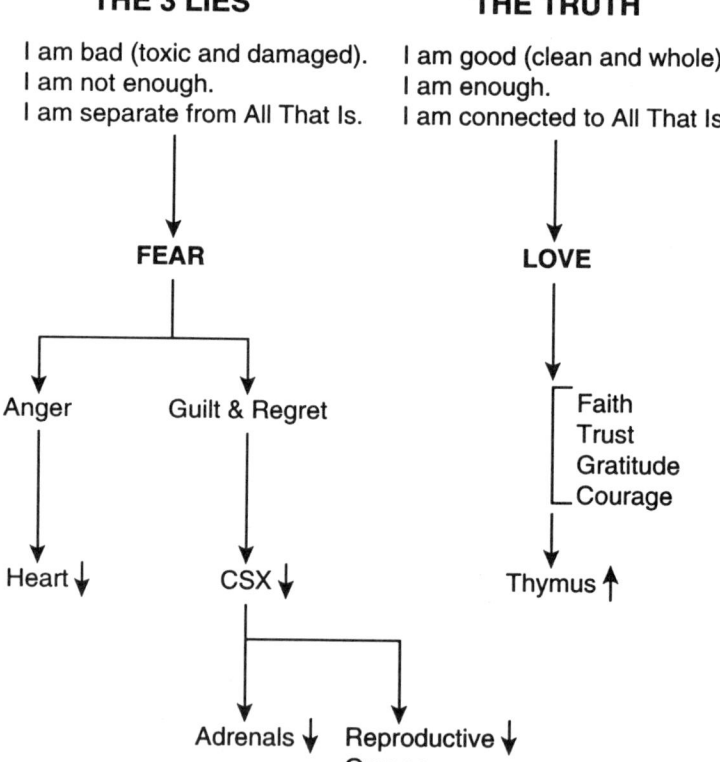

These beliefs are based on lies. (See Figure 1 on the preceding page.)

1. The lie that you are bad (toxic and damaged).

2. The lie that you are not enough.

3. The lie that you are separate from God.

Belief in these lies stand between you and your creative *Life Force*.

Stress And Disease

There is a field of energy that extends out from our hearts. Researchers have discovered that this field is continually rotating and when you experience love, gratitude and joy, the electromagnetic field of the heart opens up and fans out into the body, feeding the endocrine glands. When you experience emotions of fear, guilt and anger, this field literally collapses back on itself, pulling energy out of the endocrine system. In terms of the immune system, a high intensity state of fear, guilt or anger, will literally cause tissue damage after four days.[1] If a prolonged state of these emotions is experienced, the immune system is compromised.

The inability to handle stress is a primary factor in disease. In the case of chronic illness it is the individual, not the disease, who is in need of treatment. Stress, with all its manifest causes and effects, involves virtually every organ and chemical constituent of the human body. Stress results when we resist the natural flow of *Life Force*.

---

[1]   Kenyon, T., Acoustical Brain Research

Emotional stimuli are the most common stressors. Bio-
logically we experience two categories of stress. Reaction
of the body to situations that are stress producing is one
example. Regardless of whether the agent or situation
being faced is pleasant or unpleasant, it is the intensity of
the physiological demand for readjustment or adaptation that counts. Emotional stimuli increase the demand
for physiological readjustment. Because this demand is
nonspecific, it requires adaptation to a problem so as to
re-establish normalcy, irrespective of what that problem
may be. Joy and sorrow are completely opposite emotions and yet the nonspecific demand for the body to
adjust itself to an entirely different situation may be the
same. Both of these emotions can provoke an identical
biochemical reaction in the body.

The second category of stress is distress. "Damaging
or unpleasant stress is distress.[2] ... Activity associated
with stress may be pleasant or unpleasant; distress is
always disagreeable."[3] Stress cannot be avoided. It is
an integral part of our lives. But when the stressor is
unremitting or excessive and the body's reserves have
been severely eroded, the body begins a cascade process of degeneration. Stress then becomes distress.

With either stress or distress, there is "a stereotyped
syndrome (a set of simultaneously occurring organ
changes), characterized by enlargement and hyperac-
tivity of the adrenal cortex, shrinkage (or atrophy) of
the thymus gland and lymph nodes, and the appear-
ance of gastrointestinal ulcers."[4] (See Figure 2.)

---

[2] Selye, H., *Stress without Distress*, p. 18

[3] Ibid, pp. 19

[4] Ibid, pp. 24-25

Figure 2

The Stress of Life

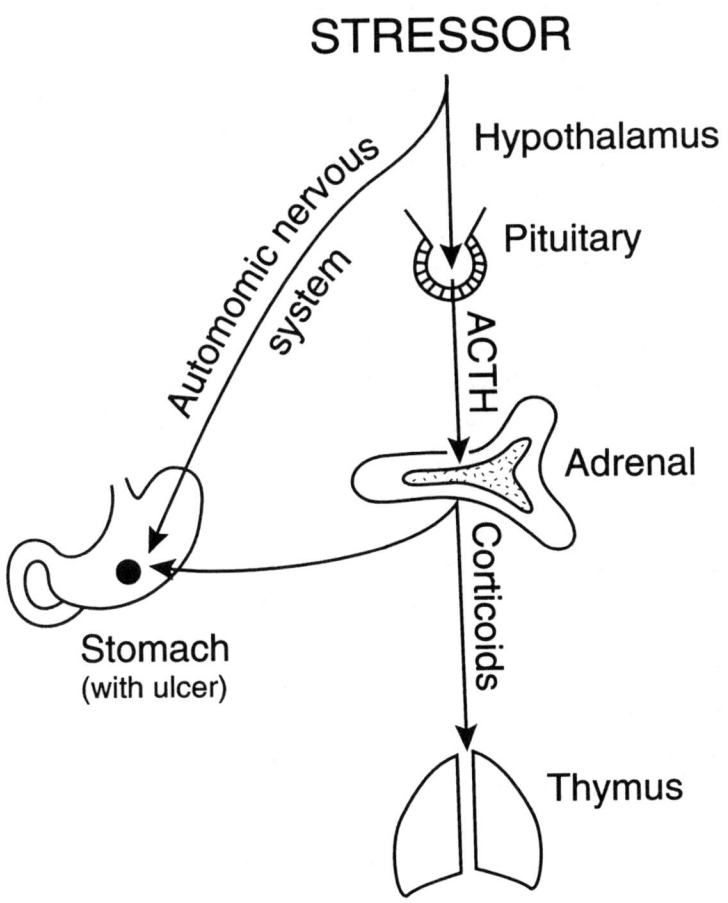

At least equally important in the mainte-
nance of homeostasis—the body's stabil-
ity—is the hypothalamus-pituitary-adreno-
cortical axis, which probably participates in
the development of many disease phenomena as well. This "axis" is a coordinated system consisting of the hypothalamus (a brain
region at the base of the skull) that is connected with the pituitary to discharge the
hormone ACTH (for Adreno-Cortico-
Trophic Hormone) into the blood. ACTH
in turn induces the external, cortical por-
tion of the adrenal to secrete corticoids.
These elicit thymus shrinkage, simultaneously with many other changes, such as
atrophy of the lymph nodes, inhibition of
inflammatory reactions, and production of
sugar (a readily available source of energy).
Another typical feature of the stress reaction is the development of peptic ulcers in
the stomach and intestine. Their production is facilitated through an increased level
of corticoids in the blood, but the auto-
nomic nervous system also plays a role in
eliciting ulcers.[5]

Adrenal glands are a key component of the endocrine
system. The same hormones that feed and govern the
adrenal glands also sustain the reproductive organs.
The kidneys play a central part in maintaining a steady
equilibrium in the body. They regulate the chemical
composition of the blood and tissues by selectively
eliminating specific chemicals from the body. The kidneys can also adjust blood pressure by regulating the

---

[5] Ibid, p. 30

production of renal pressor substances (rennin). Rennin can then act upon the adrenal cortex to stimulate its secretion of aldosterone, which also raises the blood pressure, through a complicated mechanism which is largely dependent on that balance. Too much or too little renal activity can result in high blood pressure. The body's circulatory system becomes overloaded with fluid that cannot be eliminated. Rigidity and inflammation can develop in the walls of the arteries throughout the body. Arteriosclerosis is the resulting disease commonly seen in the aged, presumably as a result of a lifetime of stress.

Fear and the Endocrine System

The kidneys and the adrenal glands are disturbed by fear masquerading as guilt and regret. When working properly, the circulatory system nourishes the adrenal glands which are the king pin of the endocrine system. During intense or prolonged stress, the circulatory system is inhibited. It fails to provide much needed lymphocytes and T-cells that nourish the body's immune system.

The liver also plays an important part in this process. It acts as a central chemical laboratory to disseminate particular nutrients. It regulates the concentration of sugar and protein in the blood. It checks and destroys excess corticoids produced by overactive adrenals. The liver also detoxifies environmental pollutants which are poisons to the body.

When a body is distressed, there is shrinkage or atrophy of the thymus, spleen, lymph nodes and all other lymphatic structures. These structures are made up of innumerable small white cells, or lymphocytes, which circulate in the blood. These lymphocytes play a critical role in the immune system. They concentrate in the lymph nodes, which are little nodules found in the groin, under the armpits, along the neck and on various other parts of the body. Lymphocytes also make up most of the tissue in the thymus and the spleen.

As far back as 1902, Dr. Fullerton, a London physician, was using bovine thymus extract for treatment of his cancer patients. In the 1950's, there was a surge of research on the thymus gland of cadavers autopsied during the Korean War. These autopsies revealed that the soldiers who had died while in battle had larger thymus glands than men of the same age who died of chronic illness in a hospital. This led to the discovery that the thymus shrinks rapidly during serious illness and great physical stress or trauma.

At the embryonic stage and in early life, the thymus gland is vitally concerned with the body's production of lymphocytes. These lymphocytes come to the thymus in an immature state from the bone marrow. Under the influence of thymus hormones, these cells mature and then leave the thymus and settle in the lymph nodes and spleen. It is there that they give rise to other lymphocytes called T-cells.

The Thymus Links the Mind and the Body

The thymus secretes a hormone into the blood stream which is carried to various organs and glands. When people harbor a life-negating, fear based thought, the vital life energy of their physical body loses its natural resistance to disease. They can easily become prey to anything from digestive disturbances to serious infections.

Cancer has become a diagnostic catch-all for the depletion of *Life Force* within the body. Sir MacFarlane Burnet, Australian Nobel prize winner, formulated a widely accepted theory of cancer. He postulated that, of the billions of new cells produced in the body each day, some of these will be abnormal. One of the functions of T-cells is to recognize these abnormal cells and destroy them. If the T-cells are not activated by the thymus gland, abnormal cells may develop into cancer. The critical role of the thymus gland throughout life is to prevent disease by activating the immune system. In all mammalian species there is a decrease in thymus activity with advancing years. Perhaps this explains the increase of degenerative disease in the elderly. The more we can stimulate thymus activity throughout life, the greater is the responsiveness of our immune system. The thymus gland is the part of the physical body that is directly affected by mental or spiritual energies. It is a virtual link between the mind and the body. A positive mental attitude promotes thymus activity.

Negative Emotions → Weakened Thymus → Infectious Diseases → Premature Death

Dr. Edward Bach was an orthodox physician practicing bacteriology at a major hospital in London during the early part of the twentieth century. Through astute observation, Bach discovered that there was a correlation between illness and emotions. He concocted seven vaccines (or nosodes, as they are known in homeopathy) for the treatment of intestinal bacteria.

He found that the seven types of bacteria were associated with seven distinct and different personalities. Based on this insight, Bach assigned the nosodes strictly on the basis of the emotional temperaments of his patients.

Bach later discovered that individuals of the same personality group would not necessarily come down with the same diseases. Instead, patients in the same personality group would, when confronted with any type of illness, react in a similar fashion. They would exhibit the same behaviors, moods, and states of mind, regardless of the disease. He deduced that different emotional and personality factors contribute toward a general predisposition to illness. The emotional predisposition to fear was the most significant of these factors. Conflicting moods which produced unhappiness, hopelessness, lassitude or resignation lowered the body's vitality and allowed disease to flourish.

Bach was opposed to injecting his patients with these nosodes. He felt certain that nature would provide a simple, natural healing system that all people could use. Along with his formal medical training, Dr. Bach used his intuition and sensitivity. He recognized that the morning dew of flowers had great therapeutic effect. He placed individual flowers on the surface of a bowl of spring water and then placed the bowl in sunlight for several hours. From these solutions, he developed 38 flower essences. He then discovered that each of these flower essences could be used as an antidote to negative emotional states and their corresponding physical symptoms. Every negative emotional state can be helped by a corresponding flower essence that alleviates it.

To quote Dr. Bach himself:

> This system of healing...shows that it is our
> fears, our cares, our anxieties and such like
> that open the path to the invasion of ill-
> ness. Thus by treating our fears, our cares,
> our worries and so on, we not only free
> ourselves from our illness, but the Herbs
> given unto us by the Grace of the Creator
> of all, in addition take away our fears and
> worries, and leave us happier and better in
> ourselves.
>
> As we heal our fears, our anxieties, our wor-
> ries, our faults and our failings, ... the dis-
> ease, no matter what it is, will leave us ...
>
> The mind being the most delicate and sen-
> sitive part of the body, shows the onset and
> the course of disease much more definitely
> than the body, so that the outlook of mind
> is chosen as the guide as to which remedy
> or remedies are necessary.
>
> In illness there is a change of mood from
> that in ordinary life, and those who are ob-
> servant can notice this change often before,
> and sometimes long before, the disease ap-
> pears,[6] and by treatment can prevent the
> malady ever appearing. When illness has
> been present for some time, again the mood
> of the sufferer will be a guide to the correct
> remedy.

---

[6] *Author's Note:* It is important to understand that the effects
of decisions made in the past are being experienced in the
present.

Take no notice of the disease, think only of the outlook on life of the one in distress. (italics added)[7]

Faith and Thymus Activation

The underlying antidote for fear, anger and guilt is faith, gratitude and courage. It is these latter attitudes which nourish the thymus gland. They actually increase the activity of this gland which is an integral part of the immune system. In every case, a positive mental attitude is the first step in overcoming disease.

Words have energy. The following words carry meaning[8] that activate the life energy of the thymus gland and fortify your immune system:

- FAITH: Belief. A revelation of man's relation to God and the Infinite. A lack of doubt.

- LOVE: Unconditional acceptance. Allowing.

- TRUST: Confidence. Relying on the qualities of integrity and justice.

- GRATITUDE: A feeling. A friendly emotion awakened by a favor received. Thankfulness.

- COURAGE: Valor. Boldness. Willingness. The quality of mind which enables man to encounter perceived danger without fear.

---

[7] Bach, E., "Heal Thyself" in *The Bach Flower Remedies,* 1931; reprint, New Canaan, CT: Keats Publishing Co., 1977

[8] *Consolidated Webster Comprehensive Encyclopedic Dictionary.* Chicago, 1957

FEAR brings Illusions
Illusions bring Doubts
Doubts bring Confusion
Confusion brings Fear

Thus the cycle of darkness regenerates itself.

PEACE brings Stillness
Stillness brings Knowing
Knowing brings Truth
Truth brings Freedom
Freedom brings Joy
Joy brings Love
Love brings Peace

And so it is that we grow in Light.

—*Anonymous*

Your Physical Body

is influenced

by your Mental Thoughts.

To be truly and wholly

Healthy,

You must awaken from

Psychological Amnesia.

CHAPTER FOUR

YOUR BODY REMEMBERS

Recollect Your Self

Thoughts affect the physical body, and the unconscious can make itself known through the physical body. In order to awaken from psychological amnesia, it is necessary to access the unconscious. You can use the physical body as a communication tool between the conscious and the unconscious mind.

Each body cell holds memory. Memories are locked in the cell walls. Your subconscious is the prison warden guarding your unconscious memory banks. The guard stands vigil in front of the cell. Your body can be a vehicle to identify and clear emotional conflicts that are the by-products of your thoughts.

Your Body's Energy Flow

According to the ancient practice of Chinese Acupuncture, each channel is an energy pathway containing a free-flowing, colorless, noncellular liquid that can be measured electronically, thermally and radioactively, and is partially actuated by the heart. In addition, there are numerous acupuncture points along these channels. (See Figure 3 for a general illustration.) These points are electromagnetic in character and consist of small oval cells called Bonham Corpuscles which surround the capillaries in the skin, the blood vessels and the organs throughout the body.

Illness, emotional stress, and toxic chemicals can reverse the body's energy flow and cause imbalances which create an environment for disease. If the energy flow on a particular pathway is interrupted long enough, the organ will cease to function efficiently.

The Chinese physician detects imbalances in the channels by first questioning their patients, then observing them and then feeling the pulses in both wrists. Needles are then used on specified points to correct the imbalance. There are 500 most frequently used points that are needled in a definite sequence, depending on the effect desired.

The Umbilicus

Of all the acupuncture points, the umbilicus (belly button) is perhaps the most noteworthy. In the center of the umbilicus is a reflex point to the thymus, which is the vital gland that monitors a persons *Life Energy*, or will to live. Prior to one's physical birth, the umbilicus is the human being's source of supply and life support. All nutrition, sensory perception and vital air supply are received through the umbilicus. After birth, this function ceases. While the umbilicus is no longer a person's lifeline, it still has tremendous importance.

Figure 3

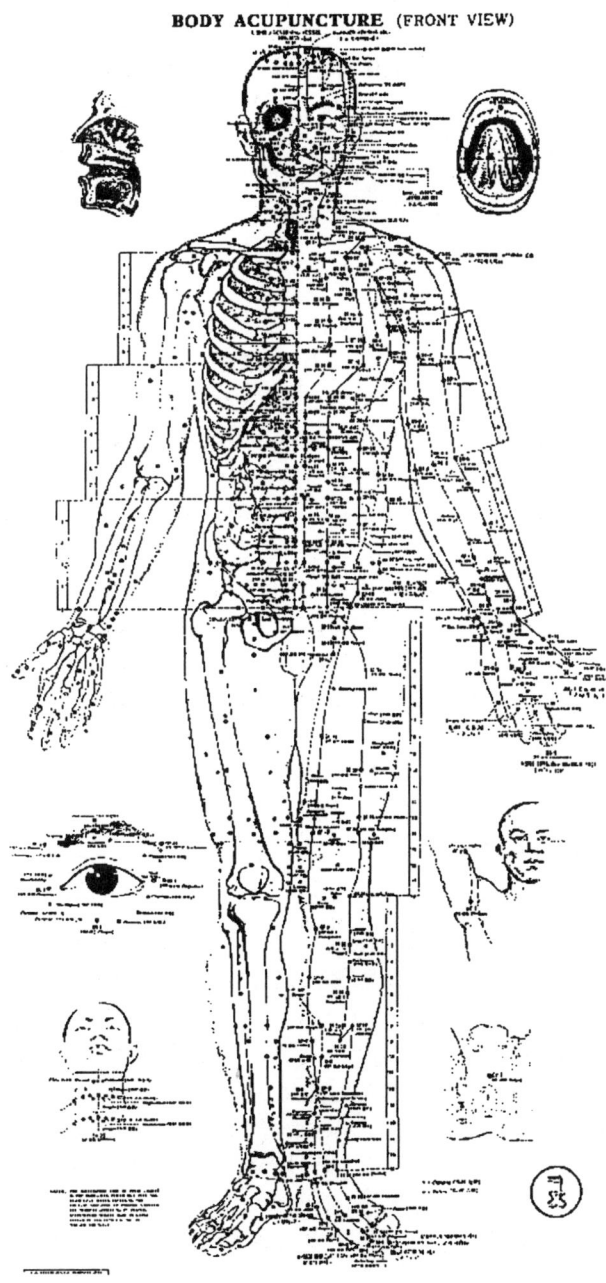

The Thymus

The thymus is the essential link between thoughts and their physical counterparts. An impaired thymus gland is the first stage of weakened body defenses. When the thymus checks weak (see Chapter 5, *New Decision Therapy*), it is an indication of diminished physical energy.

The two energy pathways (channels) that are most directly affected by negative emotions are the heart meridian, which indicates that there is an unresolved issue of anger, and CSX (circulation/sex or pericardium) meridian which is tied to the emotions of guilt and regret (to re-cry). (See Figure 4.)

Figure 4

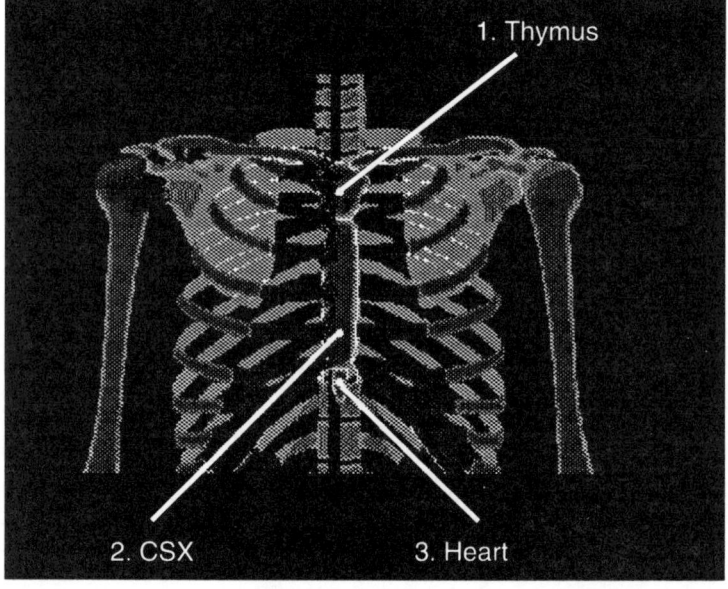

In almost every case, CSX energy is depleted as a result of a major disappointment with someone of the opposite sex. Correspondingly, the heart meridian is depleted by an unresolved issue with someone of the same sex. This could also be yourself.

There are specific points on each of these meridians that correspond to negative thoughts and can be manipulated to detect illness caused by negative emotions.

When either anger or regret are unconsciously operating in a person's daily activities, the suppressed negative energy can interfere with the electromagnetic flow of heart and CSX meridians, respectively. When there is an energy blockage in a meridian, the lymph, blood, and nerves are not being sufficiently energized. This may result in organ failure. In the case of the heart meridian blockage, a variety of medical complications may develop, ranging from mild palpitations to a coronary occlusion.

The circulation/sex meridian is slightly more diversified in its manifestations. The most obvious effect of blocked CSX energy is loss of sexual or creative energy. If the related organs continue to lack nourishment from bodily systems, they become targets for infection. Repeated infection leads to tissue damage and, ultimately, to organ dysfunction. Various forms of reproductive organ cancer are a common result.

Because we are sometimes unaware that we are fostering a negative emotion that is causing a physical ailment to erupt, we need a way to identify our deepest feelings. We need a way to communicate consciously with our unconscious mind to determine if we are harboring a life negating thought that is a precursor to illness in our body.

Communicating with the Unconscious

Applied and Behavioral Kinesiology

In the early 1960's, a chiropractor named Dr. George Goodheart discovered that each large muscle corresponds to a body organ and that a weakness in a particular muscle usually indicates a problem at the energy level in the associated organ. By strengthening the muscle in a variety of ways, the function of that organ is also improved.

The procedure of Applied Kinesiology was developed based on Dr. Goodheart's research. Applied Kinesiology (AK) uses a muscle to check the energy flow in the acupuncture channel points. Weaknesses in the muscle indicate energy imbalances in organs and glands.

The combined terms *Applied* and *Kinesiology* describe the basics of the system. It is the use of a manual energy check to evaluate a body function through the dynamics of the muscular skeletal system.

Kinesiology is the study of the principals of anatomical mechanics in relation to human movement. The Greek word *kineses* means motion and *ology* means the study of. The term "applied" puts into perspective the utilization of kinesiology for practical, concrete situations. AK offers feedback from the body itself. The insights are gained mutually between the practitioner and the subject.

Australian psychiatrist Dr. John Diamond continued Goodheart's Applied Kinesiology research, and a separate but related discipline of Behavioral Kinesiology (BK) evolved. BK uses the basic technique of Applied Kinesiology but focuses on the psychological and environmental factors in the person's life. Dr. Diamond discovered that thoughts, music, sound, light, even clothing and other people affect our bodies and our energy supply at least as much as the food we eat. Dr. Diamond researched the etymology of specific words. He determined that certain words trigger emotional responses in the body.

Behavioral Kinesiology is a method of locating energy imbalances. It provides insight into a person's internal process by correlating negative psychological states with physical maladies.

Applied Kinesiology Checking Procedure

Any muscle can be used as an indicator of the body's energy supply. A strong muscle can withstand up to forty pounds of pressure, although that amount need not be applied for test purposes.

Applied Kinesiology requires a gentle and sudden pressure to the muscle being checked. The clue to determining strength is the spring of the muscle. When the spring is not there, the muscle will visibly weaken. The difference is obvious to both the person applying the pressure (practitioner) and the person being checked (subject). A weak muscle indicates the specific point on the person's body that is under the stress of an energy imbalance.

To perform the Applied Kinesiology procedure, the practitioner uses one hand to touch a specific acupuncture point while the other hand checks the indicator muscle. This technique is known as therapy localization. (See Figure 5.)

Figure 5

Energy Checking

By using Applied and Behavioral Kinesiology, you can check the effect of a life-negating decision in both the Heart and CSX channels. AK and BK can be used to communicate with a person's unconscious mind to let you know what their body is trying to say.

Body Amorality: Denial

Both Applied and Behavioral Kinesiology can give erroneous readings, however, if all of the barriers are not removed first. Your body doesn't lie if the information has been accessed correctly. When AK reveals an energy deficiency at the umbilicus level, it indicates confusion in the body's monitoring system. There may be physical amorality which causes a person to be in denial. When the umbilicus point checks weak, the individual is not in conscious contact with their system's imbalance. Therefore, they are unable to effect positive change.

There are three layers of denial that need to be checked for before proceeding with any further body monitoring. The first layer indicates whether or not you are in communication with yourself. It reveals if you are hearing or listening to your inner self.

If you can hear what your body intelligence is saying, you proceed to check the second layer. This indicates that you are willing to let others know what is going on within you. It reveals that you feel safe enough to show who you are to the outside world (or at least to the practitioner). While we all want to be heard and to be seen, our fear of being bad or not good enough often stops us from revealing ourselves.

The third layer of denial challenges you to stay in your own truth while being receptive to another's input. Can you stay present in your truth even if nobody else agrees with you and even if others hold a different perception? To determine how to check and clear these layers, see *Checking for Denial* and *Clearing Denial* in the Appendices.

Once denial has been cleared, the diagnostic tools of Applied and Behavioral Kinesiology can quickly detect decisive "last straw" incidents. By doing this, the presenting problem goes back into circulation and a person can begin their healing. AK and BK are the first line of defense in true preventive medicine. They examine the body at an energy level and can even detect imbalances long before physical symptoms develop.

In AK, a weak muscle indicates a blockage or a constriction of the body's energy flow. Through energy checking, you can detect the hierarchy of energy highs and lows and discern which organ started the domino effect of physical devitalization.

The Body Doesn't Lie

Applied Kinesiology is a technique used to decode physical energy imbalances. It is based on the theory that your body doesn't lie. In fact, the cells in your body contain all the information you need to know as to exactly what to eat, how to treat infirmity, what exercises to do, etc., for optimal, harmonious functioning. We simply need to learn how to decode the body's language. We need to become expert computer operators in order to communicate with the most advanced computer of all, the human body.

Decide to Become Well

Negative mental attitudes interfere with the body's energy supply to the meridians as well as the specific organs of involvement. Therefore, in order to become well, we need to identify the negative emotional state that caused the problem and transform that negative emotion into a positive, energized state.

Within each of us is a balance of negative and positive energies. When a person is seriously ill, the negative life-defeating energy has the upper hand. Unconscious rage may remain encapsulated and unacknowledged in a person's psyche over a period of time. Because this ongoing anger is operating on an unconscious level, serious illness triumphs in spite of conscious efforts to ignore it.

By using the physical checking procedure of Applied and Behavioral Kinesiology, we can observe the way in which this unconscious anger works on the physical body, inhibiting an individual's conscious recognition of their condition.

When we are unaware of a deep seated anger, we begin to operate from a position of denial. The great danger with denial is that the conscious mind becomes convinced that everything is okay. The confused messages are caused by a disturbance in the innate intelligence receptors. A person persists in their self-defeating habits until a disease is so augmented that the diagnosis is apparent to all as a life threatening illness such as cancer.

The anger's ultimate manifestation is in the form of mental and physical chaos, ill health and disruption. It is the direct antithesis of the positive love energies that lead to good health and personal integration.

The will to live is paramount in any healing situation. A person suffering from a life-threatening disease at some point has made a decision to give up. That decision suppresses the immune system. The physical disease process is a manifestation of the individual's internal conflicts. When we make a conscious, positive

thought of equal impact as the earlier negative decision, we can begin to make a new connection. It's as if
we are repairing our electronic circuitry and putting
our healing energies back on line.

New Decision Therapy
Helps the Body Remember...

New Decision Therapy
Breaks the Cycle.

You can Change

at the deepest level

of your Life.

Willingness is the key.

It requires a

Conscious Choice.

CHAPTER FIVE

NEW DECISION THERAPY
A CONSCIOUS CHOICE TO LIVE

What you are experiencing today is the sum of all of your past experiences and thoughts.

Bring your unconscious thoughts to consciousness because, in the end, the unconscious gets heard and its wishes realized. So be sure your unconscious is programmed along with your conscious wishes and affirmations.

How Decisions Become Unconscious

There are a couple of reasons why you forget an earlier negative decision. One reason is that you may not have been conscious of it in the first place. Another is that a decision or a choice may have been conscious at the time, but has been put on the back burner. While it hasn't necessarily been dealt with or repaired, it is just no longer in the forefront of your active life.

Very often we know the culprits, or negative influences, in our lives and we choose to remain in a life-depleting situation. Why? Perhaps it's a fear about letting go of an unfulfilling job, a negative belief, a destructive relationship or a way of living.

Whatever the reason, we do not naturally outgrow life negating decisions. In fact, we are often unaware that we are not letting go. It can be difficult to give up these negative emotions. It is as if we have made an investment in our suffering.

Choose to Live

Letting go does not necessarily mean throwing away. However, it does mean transformation or change. It means the old computer disk is not working and it is time to format a new one. You may not have to throw out the proverbial baby with the bath water. Perhaps you just need to change the water.

Once negative life decisions have been recognized, you must make a positive, overriding decision that addresses two concerns:

- The powerful subconscious thoughts that weren't acknowledged at the time the injury occurred.

- The powerful conscious thoughts that can be recalled, but which you think no longer have power in your life.

Strengthening one's *Life Force* is the best way to conquer illness. Perceiving the true picture of one's ailing mind is the starting point.

Everyone needs light to illuminate life. Your choice to live must be strong enough to overcome your death wish or fundamental darkness. A strong life wish can bring harmonious functioning to your hormones, glands and nervous system. Essentially this requires you to take responsibility for your own life. You must be willing to look at yourself honestly and make the necessary changes.

New Decision Therapy

New Decision Therapy (NDT) is an efficient and effective, lasting way to clear previously unresolved emotional experiences that have manifested as disease and ill health mentally and physically.

NDT heals past traumas that impair our ability to move forward into satisfying career choices and healthy, balanced relationships.

New Decision Therapy helps you make *A Conscious Choice to Live*. It is about letting go and going on. It is an effective tool to help you remember events and feelings from the past that have a strong influence on your present life situation.

The technique used in New Decision Therapy facilitates the release of previously unexpressed emotions tied to the significant loss of a loved one, the loss of a cherished phase of your life, the loss of a personal hope or dream, or the loss of self-worth due to abuse experienced in the past. This exquisite therapy then goes one step further. It helps you to reconstruct your life based on a healthy and happy choice to be fully alive.

The effectiveness of New Decision Therapy is based on an understanding that physical health is the result

of a state of mental harmony. Moreover, NDT dem-
onstrates how your mind regulates the state of your
health. Many of your thoughts are unconscious and
often focused in the past. Your conscious, moment-
to-moment thoughts interact with your unconscious
mind and dictate the health of your body.

Your Eyes and the Mirror

New Decision Therapy uses Applied and Behavioral
Kinesiology to help identify precise experiences that
have weakened the body's ability to heal itself. It suggests that prior to the diagnosis of a chronic debilitating illness, the person made a negative life decision
that created a vulnerability in the immune system. By
focusing on specific emotional traumas that were not
properly healed, NDT offers healthy choices which
activate the body's immune system.

A person looks into a mirror and speaks the NDT
affirmations. Looking into one's eye and addressing
the five statements of truth to one's inner record af-
fects instantaneous reorganization.

Using the eye/mirror technique together with the
body checking procedure of Behavioral Kinesiology,
New Decision Therapy:

- identifies the moment in time when a life-negating
  decision was made

- releases the pent up emotions of anger and guilt

- creates a new, positive decision to live that activates
  the physical body's immune system.

One of the goals of New Decision Therapy is to transform a negative choice to suffer into a positive choice to live.

Sometimes people want to hold onto their negative, fear-based emotions. They use anger, guilt and unhappiness in an attempt to manipulate or pressure other people into changing. This will not elicit the desired response. It *does not work*. When a person decides to be happy, decides to live, all decisions that follow naturally create value for their lives and for those around them.

With New Decision Therapy, change can occur rather quickly. In the course of a single session, a person can journey back to the moment they began their disease process and travel the distance to a new decision to live.

Because we unconsciously write our own scripts, with appropriate therapeutic intervention we can consciously re-write them. Since we are the ones who put the attitudes into our own mindset, we are the very same physicians who are qualified to do the surgical removal. We need only to own our own lives and be willing to take responsibility for ourselves.

Some decisions may be more difficult to change than others. Perhaps the investment we have in old decisions offers a reward for which we still feel a need. Hopefully, by daring to make a new decision, we can begin to experience a more joyous life and objectively realize the limitations of our previous decision.

A person must want to be well. Readiness for healing is often expressed as, *"I've been unhappy long enough.*

I'll try anything." Human life seeks to fulfill itself. Growth is a natural process that will ultimately urge us out of stagnation. For many, pain is the calling card to joy. We sometimes have to be miserably uncomfortable before we dare to drop pretenses and misconceptions in search of self-fulfillment.

NDT: The Process

The process of New Decision Therapy consists of:

Clearing Denial	Removing memory blocks and recollecting the individuals who contributed to your emotional trauma
Forgiveness	Forgiving the delinquent persons you feel contributed to your pain
Compassionate Understanding	Recognizing that these people did the best they could given their personal histories and circumstances
Letting Go of Repressed Anger/Guilt	Releasing the negative pent up emotions of anger and/or guilt
Unconditional Acceptance	Accepting other people as they are
Going On	Moving into your own life by choosing to live fully in the present

The steps for accomplishing this are explained in detail in Chapter 8, *12 Steps to Making a Conscious Choice to Live.*

Affirmations: Thought → Word → Action

Affirmations are an integral part of New Decision Therapy. An affirmation is used to make your intent clear. As the sound waves from the affirmation travel, everything that can help you go toward your truth will become apparent. You are actually putting out the call for healing.

Thinking about the affirmation is the first stage. This is valuable, but not as powerful as the spoken word. The thought is the basis of the action. The spoken word starts the process in motion.

The affirmation clarifies the direction that you want to take. For example, a person affirms, *I am healthy.* They then begin to notice that they neglect to take their supplements. They de-prioritize meal times and frequent fast food restaurants to satisfy immediate hunger cravings. They finally become aware that they are ignoring their body's nutritional needs.

As discussed in Chapter 4, words are used to trigger the specific points in the energy checking of Applied and Behavioral Kinesiology. This tells us that words and word combinations affect our *Life Force.* They affect our energy and can show up as a weakened or strengthened meridian. Therefore, choosing words to show the intent of compassion, understanding, acceptance and forgiveness is very important. The *Life Force* is activated by the energy of the word.

Words, sounds and vowel combinations all have a meaning that stems from an etymological root. For example, the Old English derivation for the word "regret" is to "re-cry". When a person has CSX out of balance and you touch the corresponding acupuncture point (CV17) on their body, their tears will often begin to flow. A cellular memory is stimulated by the sound of the word. The mind knows. The body responds.

The affirmations verbalized in the NDT process use clean and empowering words. They are about love and acceptance. They are about understanding and forgiveness. They are about letting go and going on with life. (See Chapter 8, *12 Steps To Making A Conscious Choice To Live.*)

The words spoken are like an alarm clock with sound waves carrying particular vibrational frequencies. They help you wake up and tune in to the vibrations around you.

When you speak an affirmation, everything unlike that statement comes to the surface so truth can be revealed. Then you are in a position to make a conscious choice. Making a conscious choice to live brings up all that needs to be healed. Now you have the self-empowered choice to let go of the past and go forward with your life.

Self Discovery

In the process of self-discovery we specifically, although often unconsciously, invite partners into our lives who mirror various aspects of our yet undeveloped self. The partners we choose usually serve us to work through our childhood dramas. We may be emotionally scarred by familial relationships. We attract partners as supporting actors in our play therapy in order to heal the feelings of rejection and abandonment instilled by our less than perfect parents. When we have danced with enough partners who help us fill in the missing parts of ourselves, we begin to notice an emerging sense of self. We become increasingly *self*-referred and less *object*-referred. We begin to rely on our intuitive knowing or feelings to make decisions.

The first step in self-love is self-discovery and self-identification. The next steps are designed to include a variety of partnerships and circumstances to remember your history. Eventually, you can look at yourself face-to-face in your own mirror. The reflection now holds a whole person. Then, ultimately, the director asks for the most important piece of all, self-forgiveness. Only through self-forgiveness can self-love become a reality.

Self Forgiveness

As you use the tool of New Decision Therapy, you will come to understand and forgive your parents and significant others. You can let go of your guilt and anger over the difficult, humiliating and painful experiences that these people brought upon your life.

Most importantly, you must forgive yourself for imposing the same betrayals and abandonment upon yourself. The repetition compulsion propelled you to re-create the pain in an attempt to remember certain events and heal them.

It is time to forgive yourself for abusing yourself, for violating your physical body. You now understand that you were abused and therefore you continued to treat yourself as the meaningful others in your life have treated you.

Forgive yourself for abandoning and rejecting your genuine self. Understand that the reason for pretense and masquerade was because you believed a lie that suggested the true you was bad or not enough.

Forgive yourself for your defensive and sometimes offensive behavior. Understand that you felt threatened so you attacked first in self defense.

Most of all, forgive yourself for not trusting yourself. You did not have the support and validation you needed to feel secure. Forgive yourself for your denied feelings. Have compassion for the little person inside who felt overwhelmed by pain and hurts.

Self Love

Authenticity has three developmental stages:

- Self identification
- Self forgiveness
- Self love

Your present moment-to-moment responsibility is to recognize that which nurtures you and brings you joy. Your primary task is to give these gifts to yourself. Learning to love yourself may be the greatest challenge. It is also the greatest gift you will ever receive.

Now you are ready to affirm your willingness to be healthy and happy. You can truly operate with a Life Wish.

In New Decision Therapy, the individual is the star of their production. They have the leading role and their final act is played by their real self. While another person may point out and occasionally suggest some of the lines, ultimately, you speak your truth.

NDT is about Truth

Your body does not lie. Behavioral Kinesiology indicates what your body believes to be true. In New Decision Therapy, your body releases an old lie. It now readily accepts the truth.

The NDT process innoculates you with spiritual truth. Divine thoughts insulate your cells. It is comparable to turning the light on in an otherwise dark room.

NDT is forgiveness, based on compassionate understanding. This allows you to **let go** of toxic anger and guilt. You offer love and acceptance. You **go on** with a new reverent, *conscious choice to live*.

The Tragic Flaw

is something

you cannot avoid.

You must live its lesson

Consciously.

You can only heal

that to which

you have become

Conscious.

CHAPTER SIX

NDT: A CONTRIBUTION TO MEDICINE

An Historical Perspective

Sigmund Freud, considered to be the father of psychoanalysis, suggested that the way to break the cycle of the repetition compulsion is to bring our unconscious intentions into conscious awareness. This puts our deepest feelings back into circulation. Freud also taught us that unconscious thoughts and feelings can sabotage our conscious actions. Unconscious memories are often denied. While Freud identified the dilemma, he only offered us psychoanalysis, a long and tenuous process of self-discovery.

A century later, John Diamond, founder of Behavioral Kinesiology, developed a tool to put our conscious awareness in contact with our unconscious motivation. Behavioral Kinesiology (BK) is a body checking procedure to identify the physical effects of our thoughts and emotions.

New Decision Therapy has been developed upon these foundations. It offers a technique to help us quickly clear toxic emotional patterning. NDT uses BK to make us aware of our emotional blockages. It teaches us the most healing emotion of all, forgiveness. We cannot live in harmony if we are unable to forgive our fellow creatures *or ourselves*. NDT provides a practical method to reach a state of forgiveness, freeing us from emotional, mental and physical bondage. The result is a healing of body, mind and soul.

Birth and Development of NDT

New Decision Therapy was born in a medical office. The clinic was headed by Dr. Louis J. Marx, an orthomolecular psychiatrist. He explored the treatment of diagnosed mental illnesses such as manic depressive neuroses with diet and nutritional supplements.

I came to Dr. Marx' office as a nutritional kinesiologist. I shared my skills and knowledge of herbal medicine with him. He supervised me while I worked with his patients in these areas.

Disease and the Death Wish

With Dr. Marx's psychiatric expertise and my familiarity with alternative health modalities, we looked at the nature of disease. What is it? Who has it? It became increasingly obvious that each of the patients who were diagnosed with chronic debilitating illness had made a life-negating decision. Some event had transpired in their life which, for them, was "the last straw." Each person at that moment had made a choice to die. Many of these patients were unconsciously acting out a death wish.

Psychology is the Study of the Soul

Psychology studies the emotions. And, every emotion is held in the physical body *until it is released*. In addition to feelings, thoughts are also registered in the body. While many thoughts and external stimuli slough off in the course of a day, some thoughts and feelings adhere to the body. They stay anchored because they have previously established roots.

New Decision Therapy was born of the theory that thoughts and emotions affect the body's energy. We can find out what negative energy is stuck in the body and how it is impairing the body's optimal functioning. When a person is unaware of his emotions, they usually direct his actions. NDT helps the body make a New Decision. A person can then begin to live fully in present time.

Denial

As a psychotherapist, I observed people stuck in various levels of denial. They required mirroring. They needed someone else to reflect their feelings back to them. Trust was built slowly, if at all.

People came into my office with deep emotional wounds. Their defenses had made their lives tolerable up to that point. Now, their defenses were breaking down. The old coping mechanisms were no longer working for them. Some people knew what was hurting them. Some could even articulate their pain. Very few of these people, however, were fully receptive to medical assistance.

Until a person steps out of denial, nothing changes. A human being unconscious to their core pain cannot tell the truth. Furthermore, they cannot recognize the truth when it is expressed to them.

New Decision Therapy begins with an immediate revelation. It begins by clearing denial. This establishes the integrity of the body testing procedure. Having cleared denial, a person can discover his truth and express it to another. That person is now in a position to be helped.

I am Healthy, But...

- "...My life works as long as my addictions comfort me." Addiction is the coping mechanism of the twentieth century.

- "...My Relationship isn't what I hoped for. My intimate other doesn't see me as who I truly am. We talk, but don't communicate. We have sex, but don't make love." Do you make the other person wrong because you don't have what you want and you don't have the courage to change?

- "...Work is going okay, but I have no energy left for recreation. My creativity is diminished and my enthusiasm is practically nonexistent. Where's my Joy?"

- "...I am clean and sober. My friends say I'm somber."

- "...I don't cry much anymore. Neither do I laugh much. My life is safe and secure, but I can lose it all in a minute. I live in fear of loss."

- "...What's enough? Certainly, not me."

- "...I finally figured out there's a God, but I doubt God knows there's a me. Maybe I'm not enough to be seen and heard."

These quotes are from intelligent, responsible, hard-working people who came into my office seeking a better life. They each expressed a reason why their health and well-being wasn't total.

The Presenting Problem

A person comes into therapy and states their problem. This issue is rarely the emotional cancer that requires the psychological surgery of New Decision Therapy. More typically, their presenting problem has been thought about, shared and analyzed ad nauseam. They are very conscious of it.

In contrast, the NDT core issue is unconscious. It is an enigma driving the human machine like a drug. NDT looks for that enigma, the tragic flaw in a person's life.

Truth

Use NDT to hear and listen to yourself. Words have special meaning. They are etymological trigger points. They can affect the physical body. Choose your words carefully. Be sure your words, expressed verbally to others *and in your mind*, accurately describe your feelings.

What is your truth? Not your mother's truth; not your father's truth; not your minister's truth; not your guru's truth; not your lover's truth; not a movie star's truth; not a politician's truth. Who are you? What are you doing here?

Nothing short of the truth will register in your heart. A truly therapeutic intervention enters the heart of a person. This is the most battered and encased part of the human condition. How do you enter the heart? Directly, immediately, and surgically. This requires precision tools. NDT is a surgical implement for change. You can't "blow it." The body doesn't lie. Use the body. Clear it first and then you have an accurate diagnostic tool.

What is a Therapeutic Intervention?

A true intervention recognizes the core issue versus the presenting problem. It then exposes the buried issue and puts it back in circulation. It clears denial associated with the core issue, eliminating the need for emotional defenses. Effective therapy allows the truth to be revealed.

A THERAPIST'S DICTIONARY [9]

Therapy: The science and art of healing. The sum of measures adopted for the treatment of disease.

Disease: Want or absence of ease. A morbid state of the body or any part thereof. A depraved condition.

Emotion: A moving of the mind or soul. One of the fundamental properties of the human mind (the other two being volition and intellect).

Energy: Internal or inherent power. Strength or force producing an effect.

Therapy treats disease by clearing emotion and moving energy.

[9] *Consolidated Webster Comprehensive Encyclopedic Dictionary.* Chicago, 1957

NDT Brings Spirit into Matter

Each of us must heal the tragic flaw within ourselves. There is no room for judgment. We are all here to heal. We attend the appropriate classrooms in which we learn about our pain. Hopefully, we resolve our tragic flaw and we graduate.

We have come here to bring spirit into matter. Look for the emotion that keeps you from experiencing the qualities of peace, harmony and contentment. Herein you can solve the riddle of your repetition compulsion. We walk into the theater and turn on the projector as many times as necessary until we look into our own eyes in the mirror and ultimately forgive ourselves the lie of separation.

NDT works because it goes to the heart of the matter. It puts man's divine nature back in the driver's seat of the mechanical body. It imbues the body cells with spiritual truth.

NDT is like a Prayer

I forgive...
I understand...
I let go of my harbored guilt and anger...
I love and accept...
I go on...
I WANT TO LIVE!

You do not outgrow

a Life-Negating Decision.

You must make

an archaeological dig

into the psychology of the

Unique Individual.

New Decision Therapy

enters into the System

and

Breaks the Cycle.

CHAPTER SEVEN

LETTING GO AND GOING ON

Many people have come to me complaining of relationship difficulties. Each person believes there is a specific cause for the breakdown of communication and loss of love in their relationship.

Mary: A Marriage Betrayal

When Mary began to speak about her severe hormonal imbalance and impending hysterectomy, she believed her life-negating decision might have stemmed from any number of incidents in her life.

The events she focused on were: 1) her father's apparent rejection of her at puberty, 2) her parents' divorce when she was eleven, 3) her humiliating experience at her senior prom, 4) the birth of her mentally retarded second child, and 5) the discovery of her husband's extra-marital affair.

As we talked, she narrowed her choices to three of the events she felt were particularly significant.

Mary then stood in front of the mirror. While focusing on first one and then the other eye, we used Behavioral Kinesiology as a tool to determine the last straw event, the devastating experience from which recovery had not been complete.

Mary tested positive on all but one issue. When we tested her regarding her husband's betrayal as the result of a deceitful extra-marital affair, her arm weakened dramatically. We then began the process of New Decision Therapy.

First I asked Mary to share her story with me at length. I encouraged her free expression of all her emotions. Her feelings ran the gamut. Denial: *This couldn't be happening to me.* Anger: *How dare he cheat on our marriage.* Bargaining: *I can turn this around. I'll pretend I don't know. I'll promise to change my ways. I know I can win him back.* Depression: *I feel like I can't go on. I don't know who to blame. I feel powerless, hopeless and helpless.* Acceptance: *He really had an affair and we have some work to do to reconstruct our marriage. It may be salvageable. We'll seek help.*

In the second discussion I had with Mary I encouraged her to understand why her husband may have sought some satisfaction physically and emotionally outside of their marriage. She came to have some understanding for his response to the difficulty of raising their handicapped son. He felt the child's disability was his fault that something was wrong with him genetically. He was besieged by guilt and didn't feel safe to talk to anyone about his feelings. He created a nurturing, extra-marital love affair as an escape from overwhelming stress at home.

With real understanding, Mary had little difficulty forgiving her husband. Once she truly forgave him for the betrayal and the loss of trust, she began to let go of her regret and resentment toward him.

As she let go of the life-negating emotions that had besieged her for the last eight years, she began to feel her aliveness again. She chose life.

Jim: Release of Life-Threatening Anger

Jim was diagnosed with lymphatic cancer. He came to see me in hopes that I could convince his girlfriend to return to their relationship. As I learned Jim's story, I clearly saw his pattern of anger toward his ex-wife and present partner. As soon as the relationship developed into a commitment, Jim would become demanding and jealous. He apparently had no control over his anger. This frightened various women who would then distance themselves from him, which only served to exacerbate his suspicions of their infidelity.

Jim made no connection between his divorce from Sally and his cancer. By observing specific dates (wedding, childbirth, onset of illness, diagnosis, etc.) and checking Jim's *Life Force* (through Behavioral Kinesiology) as he reflected on these significant events, I was able to show him the correlation between his rage toward his ex-wife and his cancer.

As we talked about his past, memories and early childhood experiences surfaced to be reviewed from a conscious perspective. Jim remembered making the decision that, if his wife had ever left him, he would die. This decision was based on the unresolved trauma of his abandonment by his mother when he was six years old. He promised himself that he would never allow a woman to leave him again.

Unfortunately, when difficulties surfaced in their marriage, Jim was unequipped to communicate with Sally and express his deepest fears. Instead he lashed out at her, making home life miserable until she finally opted for a marital separation.

In the theme of repetition compulsion, Jim created the situation of his partner abandoning him in order to remember his childhood trauma. He had the opportunity to re-experience the painful nightmare of his youth when his mother blamed him for the stress in her marriage and left home. He now had an opportunity to heal the pain of his past and make a New Decision to forgive his mother and let go of the pent up emotions he had carried toward her. He went on to understand the circumstances surrounding Sally's decision to leave the marriage. He virtually forgave her for his feelings of guilt and regret over the loss of his opportunity to have a happy home. His earlier unconscious decision was sabotaging any chance of marital harmony.

After owning, expressing and letting go of his pent up anger and guilt toward significant women in his life and toward himself, Jim then had a real chance to make an appropriate choice for his next relationship. In addition, he acquired some valuable tools to assist him in the act of unconditional love and acceptance.

Illness can be a positive turning point in a person's growth process. It offers new insights into one's internal and external world. If illness is properly treated (i.e. cognition followed by appropriate responsible action) it can serve as a cause for the removal of some basic personality weaknesses. Suffering can serve as a corrective which drives home a lesson we have otherwise failed to grasp. For Jim it was a decision to let go of negativity and appreciate his life. Today he is an extraordinarily compassionate person brimming with positive energy. Indeed, he now has a strong *Life Force*.

Barbara: A New Self Image

Barbara is an overweight 56-year-old woman with low energy. She had been using potent thyroid medication under medical supervision for five years with no success.

Barbara stated that all of her problems were physical. She was certain there was a major metabolic imbalance. Applied Kinesiology revealed a number of bodily imbalances, among which a weak thymus gland was detected. I decided not to put emphasis on the thymus as an emotional factor and began by suggesting the appropriate nutritional support for her weakened systems and organs.

Barbara followed all suggestions exactly. There was certainly no reason to suspect that she did not want to be well, except for the fact that she was achieving only marginal results from all of her efforts. Of particular interest was the lack of energy in her throat center, where the thyroid is situated. I did some body work for stress release, and she began to talk.

She tearfully complained about her 16-year-old son who would not listen to her. She said their communication was completely blocked. She felt this was possibly the root of her problem. It was my intuitive feeling that the main issue preceded the birth of her son. I suggested we explore the techniques of New Decision Therapy. She was very reluctant and yet desperate regarding her physical condition. Behavioral Kinesiology pinpointed the emotion of regret and the "last straw" incident.

Thirty years ago, Barbara had married Jack, her first husband. She married him because of a strong sexual attraction and stayed with him because she "didn't want to admit defeat." She recalls the five-year marriage as being devastating from the onset. She desperately wanted children. Jack wanted a vasectomy. After six months of marriage, Jack had the operation. At that point in her story, she began to cry "for the first time" over an issue that precipitated a life and death decision. She felt hopeless. *If this is what life is about, I'd rather be dead.* This began Barbara's downward health spiral which originated with the diminishing of her *Life Force.*

We did the appropriate therapy that same day. One week later, Barbara returned and reported a definite improvement. She used phrases like, *I have more spring in my step.* She noticed positive changes in her relationship with her present husband, and even with her son, John. Also, her digestion was improved.

Barbara continued to do well for about one month. She returned for a check-up and was in the depths of depression. She was coming to grips with personal disappointments and unfulfilled expectations. This time she was eager to understand herself. She told me about her own childhood and adolescence. She was the last of several children. Her mother was 40 years old and in poor health when Barbara was born. Barbara referred to her own birth as an "accident." Her mother died during Barbara's second year. Her father, who had lived only for his wife, died shortly thereafter. An unwed sister took Barbara in and was clearly burdened by the responsibility.

When Barbara married her first husband she was going to prove herself worthy of being alive. Yet, unconsciously, she chose a man who was not really concerned with her happiness. His decision to have a vasectomy destroyed Barbara's most cherished dream for children and a happy family life. A few years after the dissolution of that marriage, Barbara remarried. This time it seemed that she and her new husband, Harry, had dreams in common. They both desperately wanted children. The tragic irony was that it took eight years for Barbara to conceive. She was 40 years old when John was born.

Barbara put all her hope into John. She was going to have the chance to prove that she could have a happy family. She decided her value as a human being rested on this. If she could pull it off, she would feel she had the right to live. Barbara's depression at that point was due to her sense of failure. John was doing terribly at home, at school and on his job. Her decision: *"If John doesn't make it, I might as well die."*

Barbara came to see me because of her weight problem, which she hoped would be resolved by proper thyroid therapy. When the thyroid did not respond to the usual type of glandular support, I began further kinesiological testing. The testing revealed that her thymus gland was at least partially responsible for the lowered thyroid function. In order to treat her thymus gland, I first had to reveal to Barbara her self-negation, or her death decision. At first she was appalled, and then she shared her story. She was relieved to speak about her hidden pain and despair.

Barbara had chosen to place her ultimate self-worth at the mercy of her son's lifestyle. John must have been feeling the pressure (even if unconsciously) that his mother's life and death decision rested on his shoulders. Barbara wanted to know why John lacked vital *Life Force*. She did not see the heavy load she had asked him to carry. No wonder he was exhausted. All of his potential energy was sapped by his mother's neediness. Meanwhile, Barbara's vital *Life Force* was tied up in her attempt to see John "make it." Both family members were operating with low thymus gland activity. The therapeutic work to be done was in recognition and responsibility. A basic life decision had to be made. Barbara had to recognize cognitively, as well as in her gut, where this drama began. Then she had to reevaluate her need for a perfect family. She could then begin to live responsibly with deep appreciation for her own life.

Vivian: Forgiveness

Vivian was a 70-year-old woman of frail stature. She possessed an elegant Latin beauty underneath a countenance that bore sadness and distrust. Her presenting problem was acute and chronic indigestion. She had already had several vital organs surgically removed. Prior to the recent surgery on a lower bowel tumor, she had been hospitalized for an appendectomy, gall bladder removal and a hysterectomy.

Vivian nervously entered my office. Her husband never stood more than six inches away from her and he did all the talking. Vivian was supposedly hard of hearing. To make our communication even more difficult, she would not look at me. She held her head down and toyed with her fingers with a slight tremor. Her husband was very worried because Vivian was not eating and was wasting away. Apparently she had been a well-built woman, perhaps even a little plump before the digestive organs became so impaired.

I respected Vivian's extreme sensitivity, while I also acknowledged the deep negativity that was robbing her of vital *Life Force*. It was immediately clear to me by simple clinical observation that medication would have minimal therapeutic value unless the patient herself decided to take some responsibility for her circumstances at that time. I explained the kinesiological diagnostic procedure to her slowly and cautiously. The initial minutes were very frustrating for all of us. Vivian continued to turn her face away from me, so that all I could talk to was her "deaf" ear! Once in a while she looked up at her husband with a snarling and confused expression. Her husband was somewhat embarrassed, and he offered many excuses for his wife's behavior.

I decided to proceed with the testing. As might be expected, I found severe energy imbalance throughout Vivian's body. The organs most significantly weakened were her liver, stomach, adrenals, pancreas, heart and thymus. The heart and thymus were the key pieces of information for me. It was natural for her digestive organs to be energy deficient, based on her symptomology. She had no heart "complaints," and she had no idea what the thymus gland was. I, however, could not ignore its significance. I knelt down to meet her eyes and blatantly asked her who was the target of her tremendous anger. She looked up at me for the first time and just glared. Her husband was somewhat shocked and apologetic. I ignored him and calmly explained to Vivian that if any degree of health was to be achieved, I would need 100% cooperation from her and that I refused to talk to her through a third party.

I talked with Vivian about New Decision Therapy. I explained what unconscious anger does to our bodies and the life-debilitating decisions we make from such a negative life condition. She began to cry quietly. Then she seemed hungry for some kind of therapeutic intervention. I made it clear that she was entirely responsible for her life and, therefore, for her therapy. I talked about stress and the thymus gland. She admitted to eating sugar all day long. She intuitively felt it might be partly responsible for her nervous irritability.

I told Vivian that if she wanted to do the work, she should set up an appointment with my secretary.

Vivian returned to my office seven days later. She was just as nervous as the first time. It seemed we were back at square one. She would not look up at me and kept turning her face sideways while continuously pulling at her fingers. The only positive glimmer was that she had, in fact, returned. She insisted that her husband remain in the room with us. I agreed to her request as long as he would sit quietly behind her and not offer any input at this session. All three of us had some challenges ahead.

I used Behavioral and Applied Kinesiology to show Vivian that her life force was low and her vital energy was so weak that she didn't have any defense for the onslaught of physical attack. She understood this as a reality, but had no hope that this feeling could change, especially at age 70. I assured her it was possible to make some new decisions once she felt and understood where the old life-threatening decisions had come from. I offered her the appropriate Bach Flower remedies for despair and hopelessness, as well as one for fear and timidity. After taking the flower essences, she relaxed considerably and was ready to do the work.

I asked many questions to which a "yes" or "no" response would give us pertinent information. By using Applied and Behavioral Kinesiology, both Vivian and I were able to pinpoint significant moments in her childhood when Vivian clearly recalled feeling her life was not worth living. She could never remember being happy as a child. Her repeated comment was, *"I wish I'd never been born."* Each time she expressed this, the tears flowed freely. Her husband was uncomfortable and probably would have tried to rescue her, but she could not see him due to her involvement with her own pain. The specific debilitating moment in Vivian's adult life was in a conversation with her only daughter 40 years before, when Vivian was 30 years old. It was 10 years later that she had her hysterectomy. Five years after that she had her appendix removed, and within another five years, the removal of her gall bladder. She had then come to our office with a diagnosis of adenocarcinoma of the colon (colon cancer). The woman wanted to die and she was finally recognizing this death wish!

I assisted Vivian in making appropriate affirmations which validated her new understanding. She was able to forgive her daughter, release the years of pent-up anger and express her deep basic love without fear of rejection. She concluded session two with the statement, "I want to live."

Vivian returned to my office ten days later. She had been taking her Bach Flower remedies and looked ten years younger and smiled warmly. She had no trouble "hearing" me, although her husband reported that occasionally she claimed "deafness" when he tried to talk with her. This time I asked her husband to remain in the waiting room during the treatment hour. They both agreed. Vivian had begun to trust me, and there was eye contact the entire time we were together.

We shared our mutual delight at her progress and her enhanced *Life Force*. I explained to her that, although we cleared the issue of a specific life-negating decision, there was a predisposition within her that was at the root of her decisions. She understood and was eager to vent the sad story of her early childhood. During the therapeutic procedures, Vivian began to build some security and comfort about life. I continued to support her strengths as she was opening the petals of her heart.

Vivian concluded her next session amidst warm tears and affectionate embraces. It was hard to imagine this was the same frail, trembling woman to whom I was introduced three short weeks before.

Vivian continued to see me periodically to deal with her physical weaknesses. Her health continued to improve remarkably. She began eating well and gained several pounds. Her physical energy deficiencies were very real, and they required the necessary physical therapy and nutritional support. The key, however, is that Vivian's lack of vital *Life Force* was the initial catalyst for the physical maladies.

Once the bodily damages have manifested, they must be treated. However, to treat only the body would be a continuous race to keep repairing damages as they surface. At first, Vivian's reproductive organs were removed. That did not make her "well." The next target of assault was her appendix. After that was removed, the gall bladder became "sick." It, too, was removed. Now it was cancer of the colon. The physical body is seldom sick first. The mental attitudes that become our life and death decisions must be treated first. The person will then have the energy to overcome physical infirmity because they are operating from the highest consciousness, the will to live.

Lois: Death and Abandonment

Lois came to my office because of her inability to control her eating and her use of caffeine in various forms. Initially, she asked for nutritional support. While her presenting problem was physical/chemical in nature, she soon began talking about her upset with her husband Sam. She complained that Sam was inconsiderate and uncaring. His major offense was that he sometimes neglected to telephone her when he would be late getting home from work. Lois was devastated if he didn't show up at the expected hour. She would eat ravenously until he appeared. She would get extremely agitated if she did not know his whereabouts. She cried, *"if he loved me, he would be there for me...he would know how much I need him."* Lois needed constant reassurance that Sam would not leave her.

The real emotion behind Lois' ranting was fear. She was terrified that she would lose Sam. When he was late, she could not stop seeing mental pictures of him in a tragic car accident. She tried to numb her pain with food and stimulants. When Lois finally acknowledged her fear of losing Sam, her anger dissipated. She became calmer and tearful. She then began recounting the day she came home from school and her mother wasn't at home. She was eight years old. The front door was unlocked and there was music playing in the house. Lois thought her mother would return any minute. After half an hour, Lois began eating and continued to stuff herself until she was numb. She sat on the couch, waiting. Her mother never returned.

At five o'clock her father came home, along with several other people. Lois' mother had been killed instantly in a car accident three miles from home. Lois never saw her mother again. There were no "good-bye's," just loss. Just emptiness.

In an effort to protect Lois, no one explained her mother's death to her.

That was the moment when Lois put a part of her life on hold. She replayed that piece of her movie every time Sam didn't appear on time. Her fear of loss overwhelmed her. She felt she could not confront one more abandonment. In fact, she had not yet confronted the original trauma. The eight-year-old girl believed that there was something very wrong with her. She must be bad or her mother would not have left her. Why wasn't she enough to keep her mother alive?

I brought Lois face to face with the truth in the mirror. Step one was to forgive her mother for dying and abandonning her when she was so young. Then Lois offered conscious understanding that her mother's death was not a statement about Lois' self worth. Lois then "let go" of her anger toward her mother for dying and leaving her. (This is the anger she had directed toward Sam whenever she was frightened.)

Lois expressed love and acceptance toward her mother. At this point, she purged the rage and tears that had not been expressed for thirty years. She was then clear to affirm her willingness to "go on" and allow for a fulfilling marriage with Sam. She affirmed her heart's desire to truly love without the threat of death continually disrupting her aliveness.

New Decision Therapy gave Lois the opportunity to live and love in present time.

Fear and Love

There really are just two major emotions: fear and love. Fear can manifest as anger or guilt. Love is expressed as unconditional acceptance.

Once a person knows the great stressors in their life, there are a variety of excuses used to remain in a life-depleting situation.

Secondary Gain

Often a person receives some gratification from a negative situation. According to Dr. Carl Simonton, a serious illness itself can offer an individual several benefits. A person may receive permission to get out of dealing with a troublesome situation. They may get attention, care and nurturing from people around them. They have an opportunity to regroup their psychological energy to deal with the problem from a new perspective. It may be an incentive for personal growth or for modifying undesirable habits. They do not have to meet their own or other's high expectations.[1]

Another reason why a person might stay in a life-negating situation is that they do not truly have access to the negative intention that they made. They may be suffering from psychological amnesia. They forgot the self-negating decision which is so deeply embedded in their unconscious and only through similar scenarios can they recreate the one-act soap operas that may bring them to the original script.

A person may stay in a life-negating pattern, marriage, job or addiction until they either become ill or remember and begin to make a new choice.

Letting Go

There are several levels of letting go. The most superficial kind of letting go is walking away. You physically detach without engaging any emotional clearing. The second level of letting go involves some soul searching. You realize that you're holding on to grievances. You acknowledge these old hurts and you choose to release them. The third level requires a genuine discharge of emotions. It probably includes tears, mourning and real grieving.

---

[1] Simonton, C., *Benefits of Illness*

New Decision Therapy addresses each of these levels.
It then begins to heal the basic emotional decisions
born of fear, anger and guilt. It reveals these decisions
through the body testing procedure of Behavioral Kinesiology. A person begins to remember how they felt
at the time they made this life decision. Once the person breaks through denial, they have the opportunity
to forgive others for the past hurts they sustained. This
forgiveness is the beginning of the person's freedom.

Honestly admitting and working through your pain
of isolation, loss, separation, or rejection, allows you
to make a conscious choice. You get to become an
artist of self-creation. Self-expression and the will to
live are essential ingredients for happiness. However,
when all of your energy is focused on personal survival, there is none left to create and to manifest your
true self.

New Decision Therapy will take you back in time to
discover the moment and the circumstances around
which your death wish was born. What was your "last
straw?" When did you decide life didn't work for you?
That decision was probably made quite some time ago.
You are in a different life circumstance today. In fact,
you actually survived that which you thought would
kill you. You are alive today! So you are stronger than
you thought. Sometimes we will not let go of our
present circumstances because we are not clear where
we are going next.

As uncomfortable as the present situation might be, it
is familiar. However, until you let go of what was, you
are not able to live fully in the present. Give yourself
permission to let go of the old and celebrate the new.
Going on can be quite an adventure. It will call upon

creativity and resources you may not have been in touch with for many years. As you *go on*, you become potent and defined. You tap into your unique, personal qualities.

However, *going on* with saddlebags full of anger, resentments and guilt is cumbersome. You must lighten your luggage. You must, in fact, *let go* before you can *go on*. Begin housecleaning now. Decide what to keep, what to give away, what to use differently and what to hold on to. Then you can bring in some new furnishings. The decorating can be fun. You can go on with a light and loving heart.

Personalize the *Letting Go* process in this book. Make it your own. Write about your hurt and anger. Become conscious of the resentments you hold toward specific people. Then find the compassion within yourself to see why these people felt so trapped and limited in their own lives.

When you have looked at the entire situation and really honored your deepest feelings, you are ready to let go of those pent-up emotions that are sapping your vital *Life Force*. Finally, you are ready to make a conscious choice to be fully alive.

The person with low *Life Force* is following an agreement to negate themselves, to die. In reality, they agree they are the person least prepared to face their own death. They want to die, but they are not prepared for death. The reason becomes obvious. They are not ready to die because they know they have not yet truly lived. The negative emotions of anger and regret have kept them in a depleted condition, sapping their vital *Life*

Force and therefore preventing them from truly experiencing their life.

Here is where illness becomes the teacher. The closer one comes to their final moments, the more clearly they are confronted with possible decisions. The more seriously ill the patient, the more immediately effective is New Decision Therapy. It appears that until the real possibility of death has set in, the patient with a death wish "plays" with the therapy. They have not yet made a conscious choice to live.

Dr. Elizabeth Kubler-Ross has worked exclusively with dying patients for more than a decade. Her message to all people is to "find what turns you on, because no one can do this for you." Her efforts with terminally ill patients highlight the essence of health. She concludes that health is being at one with yourself, no matter what the circumstances. The key is awareness. Be in the moment. Human life seeks to fulfill itself. It has the potential for growth experience from the first moment at birth until our last breath. Imminent death signals what Dr. Ross calls the pangs of "life-hunger."[2]

When a person confronts the "last straw", they may respond in several ways. They can allow their life force to wither, or they can summon up the courage to invest themselves in creative and appreciative relationships.

Each of us has a choice. We write our own script. The struggle is for personal meaning and significance. Each of us has to face that struggle within ourselves. Jim

---

[2] Kubler-Ross, E., *On Death and Dying*, p. 17

chose to overcome cancer, even though his wife had left him. He made a life decision and went on to create meaningful relationships. Barbara is in the process of learning what her own existence means. She is learning that each human being has joy as her birthright, but she must responsibly pursue her desires. No one can give you your happiness. Each person must claim it for his/herself.

A *Conscious Choice* is based on a person's philosophy, psychology and physiology. Each person is a body/mind/spirit entity. Healing that ignores one of these three parts is incomplete. The physical body expresses symptoms of dis-ease. True good health comes from one's condition of life, which finds expression in both physical and mental aspects. Moreover, we must start to view health as more than the absence of disease. True good health includes a positive outlook and the confidence to live fully and to meet challenges with *Life Force*.

The hypothesis and techniques described in the preceding pages have remarkable benefit. My goal is to bring people to an enlightened view of self. All the techniques described here offer awareness and autonomy. This equals Liberation.

A conscious choice to affirm your will to live is a conscious decision to let go of anger and to live a life without regret. Love of self will come from letting yourself and everyone else off the hook. Self love will grow naturally when you recognize the less than ideal circumstances of the past, forgive yourself and others through compassionate understanding, and release your old anger and regret, allowing for acceptance.

Stay Conscious

in the

Present Moment.

You are making

Life Decisions

all the time.

This is not a dress rehearsal.

This is Your Life.

CHAPTER EIGHT

12 STEPS TO MAKING A CONSCIOUS CHOICE TO LIVE

The Steps

Step 1:   Remember who you are. You are a part of all that has ever been and ever will be. You hold the perfect blueprint of health and happiness.

Step 2:   It is time to take a personal inventory. One by one, address the significant others who have played leading roles in your life. After each name, write down what you wanted from that person. Then, note the moment in time when you knew you were not going to get it. Compose an angry, resentful letter. Be sure to include all of your grievances, unedited. Without shame, claim your years of pain. Identify the insults. Acknowledge the betrayals. This letter is *for you*.

Step 3:   Put yourself in the others' shoes. What precipitated their actions and reactions? How were they unempowered due to their own histories and unconsciousness?

Step 4: Make a conscious choice to let go of your anger and resentment. It served you at one time. It insulated you from new experiences. It kept you safe in a cocoon spun of fear. Now you can see its dulling effect on your life. You can feel its weight and limitation. You are stronger, healthier, and more conscious now than you were at the time of those unhappy circumstances. Stop blaming yourself for unconscious choices you made in the past. Make a new choice today. Begin by releasing your attachments to old hurts.

Step 5: Write a letter of gratitude. Honor the gifts you received from each person. List the skills that you now have because of and in spite of that relationship.

Step 6: What are your personal benefits in letting go? How do you see yourself in your new circumstances? Be convincing. Where you are going on to must have more appeal to you than where you are coming from.

Step 7: Write your goodbye's. For most of us, it is difficult to say goodbye. Losing a loved one, leaving a spouse, breaking up a friendship or setting off on a new life adventure can be frightening. Anytime we give up something familiar, we experience some loss and discomfort. Often our fears block the inner voice when it is time to let go and move on. In order to really hear yourself, focus on your heart's desire and make a conscious choice.

Step 8: Now affirm your willingness to live. Acknowledge your new decision with enthusiam. It's *your* choice.

Step 9: What are you going on to? Look forward now. Dare to dream. Write it down. Recapture some of those lost visions.

Step 10: Do your homework. How will you get from where you are to where you are going? What resources do you already possess? What skills do you need to acquire?

Step 11: Words have vibrations. Your sound waves penetrate the universe. Create your new affirmations.

Step 12: Get your house in order. The doors are open, opportunities enter. Greet the day with great enthusiasm. Allow for the unexpected.

All of these exercises are preparation for your New Decision clearing session. While you can use this technique on and for yourself, it is advised to seek a trained NDT practitioner for your initial clearing. Although NDT is a profoundly straightforward process, it is easy to miss the core issue if you are proceeding on your own. It is all too common to glance away from the mirror when you don't like what you see. It is also predictable that you could miss a crucial word or turn the sentence structure around to have slightly different meaning.

Your core issue is usually well embedded cellularly. If you could have let go of it on your own, you probably would have done so by now.

You cannot harm yourself by doing New Decision Therapy. You can, however, do multiple sessions skirting the key issue. The art of this process is its incisive precision. Allow a trained person to uproot the embedded tumor within you. You can travel miles on your own from that starting point.

A reference guide to NDT practitioners is located alphabetically in Appendix G.

Remember your vision. Reevaluate your dreams
in the light of your new knowing of yourself.

Then, with no one to blame, you get to choose...
and change.

Your conscious awareness is your ticket to freedom.

The Past is gone.

The Future is being written.

Now is the time to be absolutely happy and healthy.

This is The Beginning of the rest of your life!

What feeds you?

What depletes you?

Thoughts have Energy.

Your Body listens to

your Mind.

Your Body

registers

your Emotions.

CHAPTER 9

MANIFESTING YOUR DESIRES

We see the World through our Belief Systems

We go through life reinforcing what we already think is out there, while in reality there are infinite possibilities. To effect change, we need a shift in our awareness. Once your emotional blockages are cleared, you can see the world through an open heart. You have learned from your past experiences and are living consciously in the Present. You are spontaneous, continually connecting to the Source.

A Shift in Consciousness Precedes
Physical Manifestation

For years we have made commitments to self-sabotaging beliefs. Many of these commitments were made prematurely and remain on an unconscious level, giving us a limited perspective both physically and mentally. New Decision Therapy produces a shift in consciousness. This technique allows you to exchange thoughts in your memory bank. It helps you to heal the past and see things from a new perspective.

Fear is a Dense Vibration

There is a mechanical field of energy all around us, connecting each of us to all that is. There are quantum fluctuations in this energy field. While Fear is a thick and heavy vibration, Love resonates at a lighter and higher frequency. As our awareness shifts, as our perception changes, we begin to wake up from a semi-trance state. When enough of us wake up and stay awake, our physical bodies will be flooded with the higher vibrations of love, peace and harmony.

It is time to move out of the old collective mind set born or fear, doubt and worry. Our emotions are energy in motion, creating fluctuations within and around us. Fear and all of its components (anxiety, resentment, grief, anger, possessiveness) are the end product of a lie. It is the lie of separateness. In the consciousness of love and connectedness, we know the Truth. We are psychologically free. Our physical body is simply the metabolic end product of our thoughts.

NDT Transforms Core Negative Beliefs

If you don't have what you want, perhaps you don't really want it. Maybe you have a belief that you shouldn't have it; that you do not deserve the object of your desire or the good feelings that accompany the manifestation of your desires.

First, gather up some compassion for yourself. The walls you have erected served you at one time. They had a purpose. You designed them to make yourself feel safe. As you come to know the Truth—that you are safe—you begin to walk through your walls.

The Lies

The two most toxic lies that you have bought are:
1) I am bad.
2) I am not enough.

With these thoughts in the forefront, your basic good-ness will stop you from having what you want. Your integrity would not possibly allow a diseased and bad person to delight in himself. Maybe your disease is based on the biggest lie of all, the lie that you are sepa-rate. Separate from one another, separate from God, separate from love, money and health, and separate from your beloved.

Connectedness

The ultimate cure for this made-up disease called sepa-ration is connectedness.

The addict uses his addiction to feel connected. The lover clings to her partner to feel connected. These are tiny connections relative to your entitlement. These are poor substitutes for the real thing.

The truth is that you are totally connected to all that is. Everything that you perceive as being outside of yourself is just an extension of self. You are a powerful Divine Being connected to everything that ever was, everything that is and ever will be.

A Manifestation Exercise

Inhale energy from your heart center. Bring it up through your throat, circulate love and speak the truth.

Then, ask your higher self for discernment. Be silent. Await the peaceful direction from your divine connected self. Sit in the stillness of knowing and hunger for the answer. Then take creative action.

You are now emotionally present. You can consciously choose to take responsibility for your life. True maturity involves the commitment to responsible action. It is the ability to respond with integrity in all situations. There is no more room for denial. There is no one to blame. No more bargaining. Just willing acceptance and love for yourself and others. You must flood your entire self with a higher vibration of love and acceptance.

Forgiveness

To override abuse, effective change needs to occur at the core of your being. You must come to a place of true forgiveness. This will affect your immune system as well as your creativity. The vibrational frequency of forgiveness actually raises the serotonin levels in your brain. New Decision Therapy helps you clear denial, access compassion, express forgiveness and proceed forward. NDT creates a safe place for acceptance and non-judgmental love, the true healer of all and, the greatest manifester. An old decision, conscious or unconscious, may be stripping the gears of your manifestation machine. A life-negating decision may be sabotaging your fulfillment. It is time to let go of the toxic, pent-up emotions of old guilt and anger. You can stop adhering to an unconscious psychological will left to you by mom or dad that says, "You're not okay. Don't be."

Creative Visualization

Once your conscious choice to live is activated, affirmations and creative visualization are truly effective techniques. To successfully use the tool of visualization, hold the image of what you want clearly in your mind. This will create the vibratory pattern for the image to become a reality. Clothe the picture in love. Your desire must be stronger than any fears you have on the subject. Allow yourself to be calm and rest with the peace that passes understanding. Listen with a silent mind, and you will see images, the pictures that are beneath surface chatter. Now you can bow to the mystery with humility and sweet surrender.

A Word on "Relationship"

A loving relationship is not the romantic drama that we see on the big screen. It is not the pathos of hunger, arousal and power struggle. Love is not ownership. Romantic love capitalizes on possessive attachment. A Native American Indian saying about love goes like this: *"I care about you, I want to know where your soul is going, and I hope our paths cross a lot."*

To truly love another is to accept the other being for who he is with non-judgment and with compassion, remembering ourselves and our holiness, and remembering our connectedness to each and all that is. When you become whole within yourself, there are no more hired actors, actresses and stage hands, just other whole human beings fully present to one another in each moment. Learning to love yourself is perhaps the greatest challenge and gift of all. Discover the qualities which fulfill you, which bring you joy. Then, give these gifts to yourself. Only then will you choose an intimate other based on something real, rather than an illusory need born of expectations that can never be fulfilled by another person. Once fully present to yourself, you naturally connect to others in an authentic way.

When you do come together with your intimate other, you can delicately and consciously co-create the balance of power and creativity between two equal energies. Choose your instruments and begin to play together. You have graduated from being a solo performer to being part of a beautiful symphony. And when you are ready, you can offer your music to the world.

EPILOGUE

*"Life can only be understood backwards;
but it must be lived forwards."*
                                        Soren Kirkegaard

You have just read a book about liberation. It offers you personal freedom. To be truly free, you must be responsible (able to respond) to your life. This requires conscious awareness. *New Decision Therapy* is a breakthrough in Consciousness. It is a technique that offers a distinct process of Forgiveness.

Nothing that has ever happened to you or to anyone else cannot be forgiven. Through the use of this unique tool of forgiveness, you come to a place of comfort with yourself. You begin to live in peace, trusting that your life is unfolding right on schedule. When you forgive the past through compassionate understanding, you begin to live in present time. You go beyond simply surviving and actually heal emotional traumas. Take the opportunity to do the suggested worksheets. Then seek out an NDT™ practitioner and put your past to rest.

Your life is now filled with Presence. You live in a state of grace. This is where magic happens. Magic is simply the art of producing effects by spiritual beings aligned with the natural flow of the Universe.

Enjoy your Life!

APPENDIX A

A WORKSHEET FOR MAKING
A CONSCIOUS CHOICE TO LIVE

Step 1:   **Who are you? What are you doing here? List your roles in life.**

I (your name) am _____

_____

_____

_____

_____

_____

Step 2:   **Identify the significant people in your past and present.** (Repeat this exercise for each person).

Person's name _____

What I wanted from that person _____

_____

_____

The "last straw" when I knew I wouldn't get what I

wanted _____

_____

_____

_____

List your grievances _____

_____

_____

_____

_____

Step 3: **Identify the reasons, to the best of your understanding, those people behaved the way they did.** (Repeat this exercise for each person).

Person's name _____

Why they behaved that way _____

_____

_____

_____

Step 4:   Make a Conscious Choice to let go of your anger and guilt.

I (your name) _____ let go of my anger

toward (significant person) _____

over (what happened) _____

_____

_____

I (your name) _____ let go of my guilt

and regret over (what happened) _____

_____

_____

Step 5:   Express your Gratitude

I (your name) _____ thank you (signifi-

cant person) _____ for the gifts of

_____

_____

_____

_____

Step 6:   Your personal benefits in "Letting Go" of this involvement

_____

_____

_____

_____

_____

_____

Step 7:   Write your goodbye's. Offer a letter of closure for each of the above relationships.

_____

_____

_____

_____

_____

_____

Step 8:   Affirm your willingness to Live.

I (your name) _____ truly want to Live!

Step 9: Express your vision for your Life. Without these encumbrances from the past, how do you see your life unfolding?

_____

_____

_____

_____

_____

Step 10: Getting from "here" to "there."

Resources you already have _____

_____

_____

_____

Skills you need to acquire _____

_____

_____

_____

Keep your options open!

Step 11: **Put your Vision into words. Write your new affirmation.** (Pay close attention to the words you choose.)

I (your name) _____ see (the future)

_____

_____

_____

_____

_____

_____

_____

_____

Step 12: Allow for Miracles!

APPENDIX B

CHECKING FOR DENIAL

Step 1: Establish a baseline response (resistance) by muscle checking the other person's (subject's) horizontally held arm while their opposite arm remains at their side. Apply a quick, moderate (approximately 20 pounds) downward pressure to their wrist.

Step 2: Muscle check while the subject's free hand covers their umbilicus.

Step 3: Remove their hand and place your hand over their umbilicus and test.

Step 4: Muscle check with their free hand covering your hand on their umbilicus.

Note: If any of the muscle responses are spongy (not perfectly strong when tested), do a temporal tap by lightly tapping the skull behind the rim of either ear.

If any of steps 2 though 4 checks weak, proceed to the next step, *Clearing Denial.*

APPENDIX C

CLEARING DENIAL

Step 1: Rub both of the K-27 meridian points. (See Figure 5.)

Step 2: Lightly touch the left mastoid foramen (the indentation behind the ear where the end of eyeglass frames would rest) with the middle finger of the left hand, and the umbilicus with the middle finger of the right hand.

Step 3: Switch hands and lightly touch the right mastoid foramen with the right hand, and the umbilicus with the middle finger of the left hand.

Figure 5

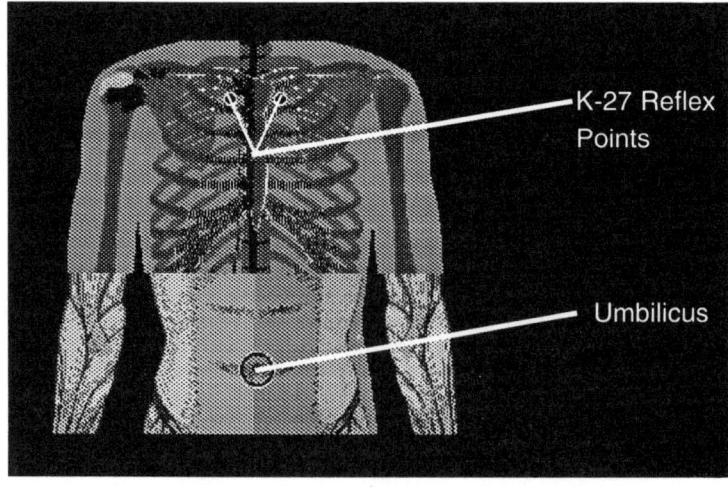

K-27 Reflex Points

Umbilicus

APPENDIX D

NEW DECISION CLEARING TECHNIQUE

After completing your 12 steps, it is advised that you see a certified NDT practitioner to assist you in your emotional clearing.

In a New Decision clearing session, the practitioner helps you focus on a specific incident and person while you look at your eyes in a mirror. The practitioner will help you choose the exact words to complete the following procedure:

Step 1: **Forgiveness**
        _____, I forgive you for _____.

Step 2: **Understanding**
        _____, I understand that you _____.

Step 3: **Letting Go**
I let go of my guilt/regret over _____.
OR
I let go of my anger over _____.

Step 4: **Acceptance**
I love and accept you just as you are.

Step 5: **Going On**
Now it is time for me to go on with my life.

Step 6: **Making a Conscious Choice to Live**
I am ready to be healty.
I am ready to be happy.
I really want to live.

APPENDIX E

SUGGESTED READING

Bach Flower Remedies. Dr. Philip M. Chancellor, Connecticut: Keats Publishing, Inc., 1971.

Coming Apart. Daphne Rose Kingma. Ballantine Books.

How to Be Your Own Best Friend. Mildred Newman and Bernard Berkowitz. Ballantine Books.

How to Survive the Loss of a Love. Colgrove, Bloomfield & Williams.

Immunology, Aging and Cancer. Sir MacLane Burnet, San Francisco: W.H. Freeman and Company, 1976.

Love, Medicine and Miracles. Dr. Bernie Siegel.

Magical Mind Magical Body. Dr. Deepak Chopra, Nightingale Conant (audiotape series)

Once My Child...Now My Friend. Elinor Lanz. Warner Books.

Questions and Answers On Death and Dying. Dr. Elizabeth Kubler-Ross, New York: MacMillan Publishing Co., Inc., 1974.

The Stress of Life. Hans Seyle, M.D. McGraw-Hill Book Co.

Your Body Doesn't Lie. John Diamond, M.D. Warner Books.

APPENDIX F

CERTIFIED NEW DECISION THERAPY PRACTITIONERS

As of this publication, the following is a list of certified NDT practitioners. For additional practictioners in your area, please contact Kandis Blakely at (916) 926-0622.

Anthony, Sylvia G., DD. Altadena, California. (818) 798-4620

Becker, Norma. Ontario, Canada. (905) 859-4561

Belleci, Katherine. Holualoa, Hawaii. (808) 324-6210

Bernhardt, Jane. Fairfield, Iowa. (515) 472-5763

Bordman, Royce. Bryan, Texas. (409) 696-2031

Brooks, Jim. Houston, Texas. (713) 524-3905

Brunell, Sally, MS. Salem, Oregon. (503) 390-2201 or
    1-800-336-6450

Campbell-Schneider, Candice. Fairfield, Iowa. (515) 472-7737

Castellano, Gina. Houston, Texas. (713) 521-7037

Clark, Melanie, MFCC. Lafayette, California. (510) 283-7157
    and Benicia, California. (707) 746-0122

Coleman, Elizabeth, MA, MPA. Mt. Shasta, Calfornia/
    Klamath Falls, Oregon. 1-800-936-6442

Con, Elsa, PhD. Carmel, California. (408) 622-9114

Conna, Steven. Fairfield, Iowa. (515) 472-3664

Crocker, Mark. Monroe, Oregon. (503) 847-5201

D'Alterio, Paul. San Francisco, Calfornia. 1-800-936-6442

D'Angelo, Jenny. Santa Cruz, California. (408) 426-0520

Davis, Jacqueline. Fairfield, Iowa. (515) 472-9642

Douglas, Barbara. Seattle, Washington. (509) 996-3995

Hall, Jé-Ru. Fairfield, Iowa. (515) 472-9130

Jongeward, Lila H. Fair Oaks, California. (916) 961-0245

Jongeward, Nancy C. MA/MFCC. Sacramento, California.
    (916) 482-9201

Jongeward, Paul A. EdD/MFCC. Fair Oaks, California.
   (916) 966-7740

Kawahara, Lisa. California & New Jersey. (500) 437-5472

Keene, Sheila. Fairfield, Iowa. (515) 472-9130

Kiggins, Carol. Estacada, Oregon. (503) 630-3590

Kuehnemann, Aron. Fairfield, Iowa. (515) 472-9642

Lengyel, Andrea, BS. Milwaukie, Oregon. (503) 659-3294

Lester, Lucinda. MA/MFCC. (916) 483-6440

Lile, Tom, MD. Minneapolis/Wisconsin. (715) 386-1154

Mandis, Mary, Ed.D. New York City, New York.
   (212) 769-9309

Nandi, Jaya Ki, MS. Big Sur, California. (408) 625-0775

Nicholas, Sandra. Houston, Texas. (713) 522-0990

Owers, Betty. Miami, Florida. (305) 233-8226

Pera, Jan, MFCC. San Francisco, California. (415) 346-9320
   or (510) 283-4023

Phillips, Michael George, DD. Los Angeles, California.
   1-800-852-4372

Price, Nancy. MA/MFCC. Oakland & San Francisco, California. (510) 834-0401

Rabe, Mary Sue. College Station, Texas. (409) 696-2031

Ramsey, Nettie. Houston, Texas. (713) 984-9435

Ringermacher Fox, Celia, MA. Fairfield, Iowa. (515) 472-9437

Robb, Rob. Carmel, California. Nationwide 1-800-887-7622

Sanchez, Teah. Monterey/Santa Cruz, California.
   (408) 483-3501

Schmit, Donald. Fairfield, Iowa. (515) 472-5481

Scruby, Rusty. Keizer, Oregon. (503) 390-1880

Tart, Ellen, D.Sc. Escondido, California. (619) 738-6135

Tugmon, Tabatha. Houston, Texas. (713) 621-8467

Vogel, Nadji. Salem, Oregon. (503) 394-3551

Warf, Sara. Houston, Texas. (713) 852-4485

Wassbauer, Hubertina. New Zealand. (03) 476-1338

White, Rosemarie, CR. Florence, Oregon. (503) 997-4289

Wood, Cheryl A. Bellevue, Washington. (206) 865-9662

Zatoon, Zae, PhD. Kailua-Kona, Hawaii. (808) 325-0222

FOR FURTHER INFORMATION
on New Decision Therapy™ Training and
Certification Courses, contact:

Kandis Blakely
c/o Atherika Productions
P.O. Box 1091
Mt. Shasta, CA 96067
U.S.A.

To order additional Books and Tapes,
send check or money order with order form below.

Title	Price	Qty.	Total
Your Body Remembers A Conscious Choice to Live	13.95		
New Decision Therapy; NEW 1996 30 minute video	29.00		
Shipping & Handling: $4.00 for first item; $1.25 for each additional item			
Calif. residents add 7.25% sales tax			
	Total		

Mail to: Atherika Productions
P.O. Box 1091
Mt. Shasta, CA 96067
U.S.A.